The ROLLING STONES
THE LAST TOUR

PHOTOGRAPHS BY
PHILIP KAMIN
TEXT BY
PETER GODDARD

Beaufort Books, Inc.
New York Toronto

Design/Martin Soldat

Beaufort Books, Inc..
9 East 40th Street,
New York, N.Y. 10016

Library of Congress Cataloguing in Publication Data

Kamin, Philip.
The Rolling Stones.

1. Rolling Stones. I. Goddard, Peter.
II. Title.
ML421.R64K35 1982 784.5'4'00922 82-4572
ISBN 0-8253-0118-1 (pbk.) AACR2

Philip Kamin used Canon cameras, Ilford film and paper, and Kodak color film. Film products, and development and prints by Allan Stokell, C.J., Don, and John Rutledge, from Positive Images, Toronto, Canada.

Printed in Canada

10 9 8 7 6 5 4 3 2 1

The ROLLING STONES
THE LAST TOUR

ACKNOWLEDGMENTS

For Bella and Willie.

Very special thanks to Art Collins, Alvenia Bridges, Cathy McGinnity, Paul Wasserman, Greg Gadson, Joe Seabrook, Jane Rose, and, of course, the Rolling Stones.

This book could not have been done without Allan Stokell and Positive Images, Robert Bonneville, Jim Williamson, Tom Berry, Kim Mitchell, Dean Motter, Gary Muth, Kevin, Mike Lahr, Bruce Carter, Phil Collins, Peter Gabriel, and Chester Thompson.

I would also like to thank Debbie Haxton, Ian Grant, Brenda Jones, Q107, *Music Express*, Bruce Erskine, Paul Faberman, Ed Ferris, Willie and Sylum, Steve Howard, Danny, Igor, and all at CPI, Tony Levin, Brad, Joey, John Small, Lee-Anne, Dave Kirby, Wilder Penfield III, Liam Lacey, Jim Rooney, Rick Ringer, The New Music, Larry's Headspace.

Thank you as well to my parents, Stephen and Michele, grandparents, Bernie and family, Emma, Marlene, and Joe, and Morris and Helen.

P.K.

Thanks to Paul Wasserman, David Pritchard and Alan Lysaght of Sonic Workshop, the Rolling Stones, and Carol Ann.

P.G.

Chicago, Ill.

They are waiting on the shingle—will you come and join the dance?
Will you, won't you, will you, won't you, will you join the dance?
Will you, won't you, will you, won't you, won't you join the dance?

Lewis Carroll, *Alice's Adventures In Wonderland*: A Lobster-Quadrille.

Rockford, Ill.

I The sky is howling in Hampton, Virginia, the night The Rolling Stones' Tour of America ended. The band is long gone, the crew is packing up. U.S. Air Force jets are whining over nearby Langley Air Force Base, and a harsh and bitter wind is bringing winter down out of Canada into Chesapeake Bay. It's December 20, 3:50 A.M. my watch says. I can't sleep. And it's not because of the noise.

The last tour. That's what is going through my head. It may be not just the last tour for the Rolling Stones in America, it may be the last rock tour that will really matter—the last one, that everybody, even people outside of rock'n'roll, wanted indelibly etched in their memories.

I'd followed it in part, since it rolled out of the dark, farming country fields of Brookline, Massachusetts where the Stones rehearsed before opening in Philadelphia, in September '81. And I've been waiting for the crunch to come, that bit of madness or weirdness or outright chaos that usually follows at the Stones' heels like a mean little black dog: a hotel room smashed, a paternity suit, a fight between Mick Jagger and Keith Richards—*anything*.

But no. It's not the way things have worked out this time around. Buffalo. Kansas City, Seattle, Orlando, New York. Fifty shows and...nothing. There's no boozy bustup for Bill Wyman's 45th birthday in Orlando, Florida. Instead, everyone jets in to float happily on a rented boat in Disney World, five mil-

Rockford, Ill.

lionaires, pleasuring themselves as they approach middle age.

And that is what's disturbing, what *doesn't* happen. It's like hearing that awesome silence before a storm—but a storm which never comes and a silence which won't stop.

I head down the hall of the Hampton Sheraton, looking for a drink or whatever else is available. I know I'll never see sleep this night, for something has gone I thought would never leave. After the European segment of their tour, this past summer, the Stones may yet go out on the road again—having grossed some $50 million in America alone this time, how could they afford not to? But this will be the last time that it will matter as much as it does now—and in the way it does.

As good as the album *Tattoo You* is, and as many millions of copies it has already sold,

Rockford, Ill.

the Stones weren't zigzagging across the continent to be listened to. They were there because they were needed; they were the last connection with the '60s and with what rock once was. It was the crowds, which grabbed up every ticket for every show, which kept this tour going, not the music. The band went along for the ride. And Jagger knew it, too. Jagger knew that he and the others had become a projection of everyone's fantasies. So he played the role. They *all* played the role. They played being the Rolling Stones.

Making a wrong turn in the nearly pitch-black corridor, I almost fall into a swimming pool. The party has moved elsewhere but a hundred or so dark-green Heineken bottles are floating in the chlorine-green water and one of the band's crew, a hulking roadie in a khaki flack jacket, is trying to sink them by throwing candies at them.

We glare at each other. He looks depressed, I think.

"Sad it's all over?" I suggest as — *bing*! — he hits another bottle.

Bing!

"Naw," he says, still sullen.

Silence. "Tired?"

Boing-bing.

He nails two in one shot.

"I'm feeling nothin'," he says slowly. "I'm just waiting for my check."

The *Daily Press*, "Hampton Roads' Morning Newspaper," is full of concern about the concerts here. "One quick item which really bugs the life out of me is the extensive radio hype," goes one letter. "Stations want their listeners to believe the petitions they signed were the major factor in bringing the Stones here. This has to be the greatest snow job since 1969."

And another: "This was a soldout concert and our children, standing in long lines on a very cold day, were turned away, probably as Washington D.C. folks were making purchases."

And finally: "It was amazing to read recently of 26,000 tickets to the Rolling Stones' concert being snapped up within not even three hours at $15.75. Indeed, in tight economic times, I was surprised that such money

Detroit, Mich.

New York, N.Y.

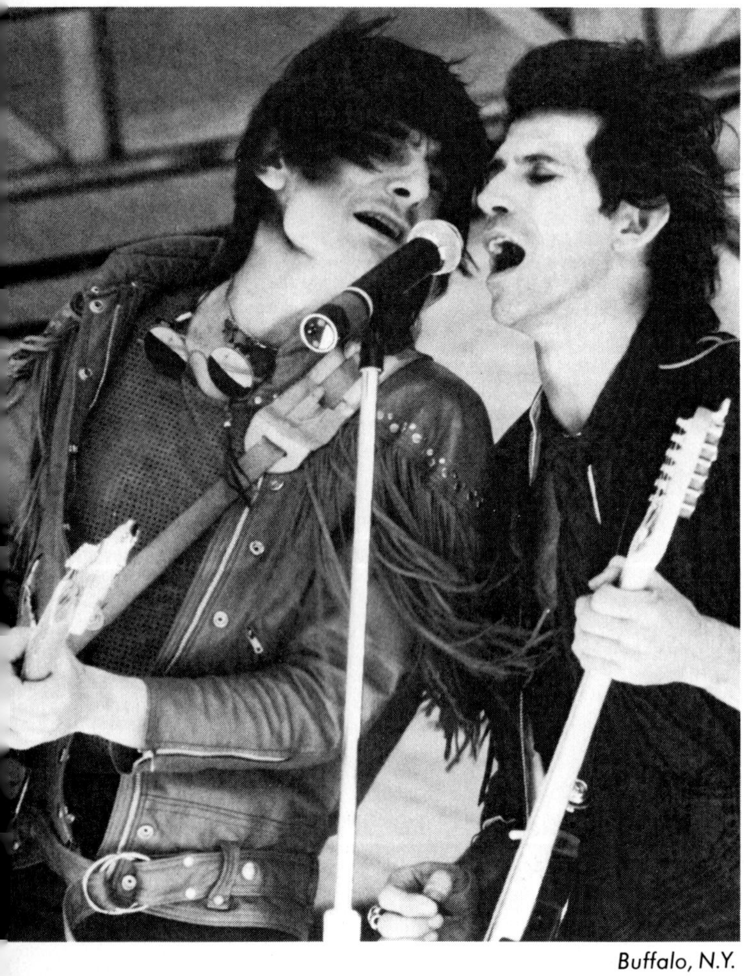

Buffalo, N.Y.

was circulating locally! Everyone is certainly entitled to their own interests and diversions, but it is a true shame that local public libraries and bookstores don't enjoy the same mass level of patronage as such 'events' as a rock concert. It says a little about youth's priorities, finally and otherwise. But, as I said, each to his own. Lest a critic replies about the great economic spinoffs from the Stones' local appearance, I am aware of that and it is, of course, good for area business. I am not so critical as I am stymied at the huge numbers involved."

2

For his last night onstage in America, Mick Jagger is given somewhere to run.

A slim, curving platform arcs out from the stage and halfway down both sides of the Coliseum. With this, a remarkable shot is provided for the camera crews, shooting this for closed-circuit cable television—it's being beamed into 17 cities with some 800,000 people seeing it—and for the concert movie. They'll have him running and running and running, and always with a crowd behind him. Jagger isolated is one thing, Jagger with people behind him is entirely another. Without a backdrop, he seems huge—physically larger than he is, solid, menacing, imposing. With a crowd, he diminishes in some ways: he's funnier and rubbery, kidding, fooling around. With a crowd behind him, he's great theater.

Giving him this stage meant something special. It meant satisfaction. Then again, that's exactly what this entire tour has been about and why the momentum it had gathered through America rolled it high, wide and spinning happily into Europe the following summer. Satisfaction. The Stones getting what they wanted. Audiences getting what they needed.

The crowd here, easy-going and in a party mood—the Stones had let it be known early on they wanted everyone to dress up—wandered in and around the camera equip-

Rockford, Ill.

ment as if they were exotic stalls in a Victorian street fair. I wonder at the possibilities of this enormous stage yet I notice that everyone else is treating it as if it were to be expected. I suddenly realize why: most people here have never seen the Stones before. However, having heard repeatedly about their reputation as "the greatest rock'n'roll band in the world," they have come to expect what I see as an added bit of the spectacular. Why not —it's the Stones, right?

Rock has never been fully comfortable on the concert stage. The music is too big (an unwritten law seems to be, build a bigger stadium and more powerful amps will come along to fill it) and the players too small. The stage has been accepted only in passing. Rock grew up on tiny raised platforms—they could hardly be called stages these—on floors in pubs, clubs, juke joints and dives, in the back of community buildings and across corners in legion halls. Now it's ending up on space-vision video.

And along the way it grew too big, theatrically and musically, for the platforms it had to work on. The stage that dwarfed the Beatles in due order came to seem to be too small for Alice Cooper or Emerson, Lake & Palmer. Rockers I've talked to along the way, Sting of the Police for one, have felt the need to go beyond the limitations of the stage. The passion for video, especially among musicians, is more than an exploration of a new technology.

Detroit, Mich.

Denver, Colo.

Video, cheaper and more accessible than the the movie screen, gives the rocker the ability to imagine and realize his act on any physical scale and in any fantastic setting he or she wishes. But video is as much a symptom of this need to expand as it is an answer for it. The development of music video reflects rock's frustration with the means it has to work with, and frustration has always been super-charged jet fuel for rock. The music thrives on frustration. Until now. Now the Stones, the ones who defined that frustration in (*I Can't Get No*) *Satisfaction*, look like they're getting what they want.

"You've seen the Stones before?" asks the girl with a leather vest and braided hair, a sort of Bo Derek meets Hiawatha. She was, I figure, about 14.

"Oh, I guess about 1966," I mumble, preoccupied by what's around.

She seems awestruck. "But that's even before they were disco," she says.

She hadn't heard me correctly and thought I'd said 1976. Reluctantly I explain: "No, sixty-six—you know, ten years before that."

I realize I could just have easily have said 1066.

A curious thing is happening—the crowd pouring in from outside is forming two audiences, one inside in the center ring by the stage, one outside, each part of the other's show. George Thorogood, the Stones' opening act for much of this tour, thumps onstage

Chicago, Ill.

and for a moment everyone starts watching how everyone else reacts.

He's the Stones' connection with their own past—the blues. A guitarist in a bar band most of his adult life, he suddenly found himself increasingly popular as the result of several potent blues albums he'd made for Rounder Records, a small independent record company. Starting in San Francisco, critics across the country each in turn "discovered" him, and through him were reminded what rock's rib-rocked basics were all about.

In Philadelphia, at the very beginning of the tour, I'd happened to find Thorogood by himself backstage. He'd just finished playing to 90,000 people, the biggest crowd he'd ever seen in his life.

"So, has there been any move to have you play with the Stones?" I asked, thinking about backstage jams and what a natural combination he and Keith Richards might be.

"That would be... would be amazing." He grinned a goofy, sweet grin. "Like going on a date with Brigitte Bardot."

His sound's enormous; blues taken to the Nth degree. Yet for most of us he remains a tiny dot cavorting on the distant stage, until he starts moving down the side stages. It wasn't that many years ago when he was playing in places so small people at ringside tables could reach out and grab his leg. "And that," as Keith Richards once told me, "is when you

Syracuse, N.Y.

really know you're playing to people." No wonder Thorogood needs to always get closer to those hands waiting for him there. What real wonder is that the Stones, after twenty years, still feel the same need.

The rock stage has been limiting in a psychological way, too. The tension in the best shows has always been basic: How close could the musicians come to the crowd? How close would they come to being wrapped up in the same feeling as the audience? How close could the two sides come to one another? How near was the unity—as close as any kid playing a favorite song over and over until its part of his or her thinking?

Likely this is why some of the greatest of the rockers always managed to find some way of getting *off* stage—Bruce Springsteen's sweet, thrusting leaps into the outstretched hands of his fans; Chuck Berry sticking the neck of his guitar out over the stage daring anyone, everyone, to grab it; or George Clinton, in the early days of the group Parliament Funkadelic, running into a crowd packed into a Detroit hockey hall wearing only feathers, and everyone around clutching and plucking and laughing away. The stage was only where the show *started*. It ended out there, in a clutch of hands, in the crowd.

This stage was for Jagger, then, what the entire tour had been for the entire band—a true luxury. Satisfaction.

No one was expecting this, neither the Stones nor Stones' fans. But there's never been another time for it. This, everyone senses, could well be the last tour. And so there was no holding back. Satisfaction was wanted and satisfaction gained. Yet the very idea of satisfaction goes against the grain of rock'n'roll. Rock was always a small "us" against a much bigger "them." It still seems this way even though many of us who still love rock—and more than half the people who showed up to see the Stones—have become, as the cliché goes, the very people who rock opposed. It still seems this way even though there is something called a rock industry, worth *billions* of dollars. It still seems this way because...well, because despite every attempt (many which have been successful) to homogenize rock for broader, less committed consumption, rock is still used not just for entertainment but for the catharsis.

Despite its need to push beyond the limits—and despite the idea held by those who don't care much about it that rock, almost by definition, means excess—rock is, essentially, a music of satisfaction denied. A deal with the devil has gone down: the more rock wants the more it needs.

So the Stones, despite real and rumored wealth, still remain in the opposition; to what exactly will never be completely clear—maybe like Peter Pan, they're against nothing more than growing up.

They're still the outsiders. Somehow they've never fit in even though their backgrounds are as bourgeois as anyone's. They're only tangentially political and only then when sex seems to be the issue. They've been described (sometimes rightly but for many of the wrong reasons, I think) as decadent. For all this, Keith Richards's grin is a true rebel grin, all sassy and naughty and hinting and heaven-knows-what.

For this to lead to the acceptance that brought them this far, is not beyond comprehension. It was beyond expectation, though.

Suddenly, they're here. Live. In person. Onstage.

They're introduced and it doesn't quite work. It never has. Their stage set, designed in pastel colors and enormous broadly-drawn sketchwork, is a vast cartoon. They're produced out of it like other cartoon characters, not quite real. And you can tell it in the way everyone reacts, the first cheer sounding rock-concert obligatory ("Yeah!!! Get it onnnnn!"), then the second, richer, more thrilling and obviously more deeply felt coming when it was understood exactly who the first cheer was all about ("It really is, I mean, it's them, the Stones!").

There's the low rumble of Bill Wyman's bass falling down the minor scale ladder of notes beginning *Under My Thumb*. To me, it has always been one of the greatest of the less-played Stones' pieces, one of the key elements in one of rock's great albums, *Aftermath*, out in 1966, when the Stones had begun to wean themselves from their blues-based leanings and when they were beginning to come out from under the Beatles' shadow. It is, in this light, one of the first true Stones' songs—and one of the more theatrical. Keith Richards and Ron Wood ride this bass line down, adding the backbeat, and suddenly there's Jagger, shouting lyrics at the crowd.

He leaves great gaps between the words which create an enormous tension. The Jagger-Richards songwriting team never aimed for the kind of completeness Lennon-McCartney did. Beatles' songs sit well on the page: they look like songs, the way something by Stephen Foster looks like a song, something you can play at home on the parlor piano. A Jagger-Richards song needs a rock performance to complete it, where the high-level play of tensions works best.

Jagger keeps to the middle of the stage, backing away from the crowd it seems, yet taunting it. The great sweep of the stage is ignored for the moment. Jagger is pure voice.

Long before this tour began, several feminist organizations launched campaigns against the Stones, the Stones' tour, and even Stones' songs, *Under My Thumb* in particular, saying they were sexist and anti-women. For the most part the Stones ignored the protests and went on as planned. Along the way what mild opposition there was died down, not that the original attack was completely off-target, though. *Under My Thumb* is not likely to end up in the Mz magazine song book, even though it's not about women but about a woman, and it does deal in hate as much as it deals in revenge.

If the Beatles took the high-road in the '60s, the one that wound around all the dreams we now think are lost, the Stones headed straight to the low-road and found there what might be the final legacy of the '60s—the gathering

Denver, Colo.

power of women. Stones' songs are drenched in sex. It's a lustiness that comes from close combat.

They began this tour so loose everything almost fell apart in the first Philadelphia show in September, 1981. That much looseness was a miscalculation. They're still loose tonight, near the end of it all, and it's a looseness that's calculated. Richards stands to Jagger's left, with Bill Wyman slightly behind. To Jagger's right there's Ron Wood, while behind, Charlie Watts is hunched over his drum kit. However else they interact—Woody stumbling up to the mike, arms and legs perpetually akimbo, or Richards moving near center stage for a solo now and then—together they act as one enormous slingshot for Jagger.

He returns to them to start a song, but once it's underway its rhythms shoot him up along one side of the Coliseum or another, the great craning neck of the overhead camera zooming in as he rushes by, the people behind him a blur.

He's running, picking up speed as he goes. And whenever he stops, he starts dancing—dancing out of reach. Only fifteen minutes into the show and he's shed his athlete's warmup jacket and is completely drenched in sweat. And the music, which had a kind of wobbly dignity at the beginning of the tour, now springs out as if it were part of some hidden clockwork that was wound up too tight.

When The Whip Comes Down. It's nearly impossible to separate what Charlie Watts and Billy Wyman are doing. They're pistons in a well-tooled machine.

This night, like most on the tour, is a retrospective. And the concert album, *Still Life*, only the band's fourth live album and the first since *Get Yer Ya-Ya's Out* in 1970, confirms the retrospective intentions: following *Under My Thumb* comes *Let's Spend The Night Together*, *Shattered*, *Twenty Flight Rock*, *Going To A Go-Go*, *Let Me Go*, *Time Is On My Side*, *Just My Imagination*, *Start Me Up* and finally, *(I Can't Get No) Satisfaction*.

What this is all about, is a retooling of the band's past for current consumption. *Start Me Up* is filled with its own great dramatic starts and stops and begins with a guitar riff that has the majesty of an anthem—in short, a song which, although relatively new to the band, fits neatly into the best work they were doing in their fertile mid-'60s.

And then there's Mick Jagger, somewhere just over my head, dangling dangerously out of a crane above everyone's heads. As he's

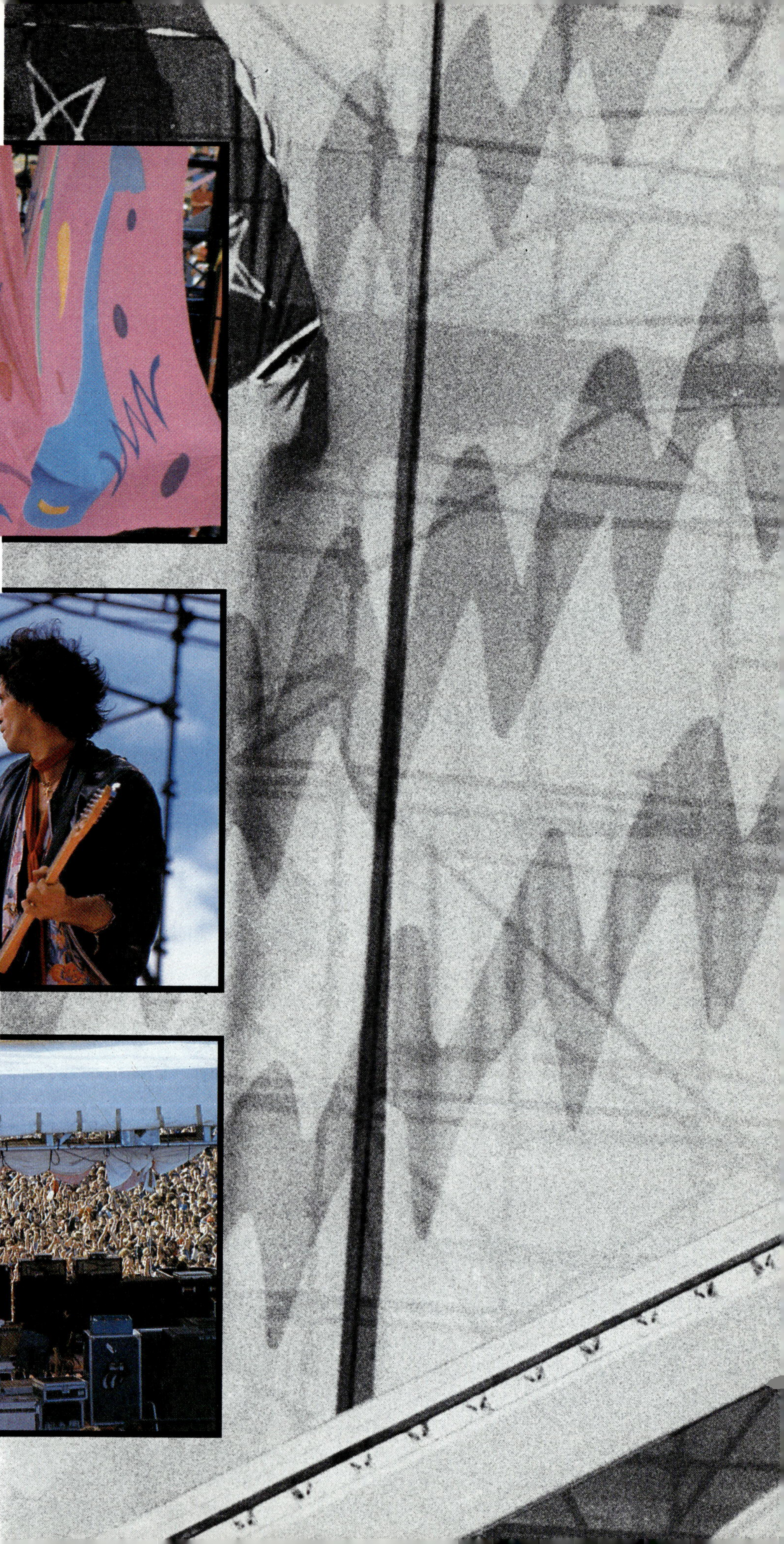

Philadelphia, Pa.

Denver, Colo.

Denver, Colo.

Buffalo, N.Y.

Buffalo, N.Y.

running up and down this long arc of a stage, people hold out their hands to touch him as he goes by. But they never do. They're always too late and he's by them before they know it.

He used to dance. Now it is a dance *with athletics*. It's not vintage Jagger, but something new — Jagger revved up into high gear.

The new Jagger onstage has changed him somewhat. At least, it's changed the way he's treated. It's taken some of the threat away, the purely sexual threat. America may have defined itself in terms of its masculinity but it's been terribly restrictive in what it considers proper roles for men. And until now, Mick Jagger has never suited America's idea of what a man was all about.

What shocked the country about Jagger was not, in the end, his long hair or his pouty, salubrious lips or his androgeneity, although those certainly cut hard across the grain. (I still can remember staring at the cover of the *Big Hits* (*High Tide and Green Grass*) album, trying desperately to find some clue if they were, indeed, gay or not. If one day I was convinced one way, the next I was convinced the other.) What was really upsetting was what he did with his body.

This has always been the cutting edge in rock roles, even way before Elvis's pelvis — what men did with their bodies. There's no formula in what Jagger does — at least not one that is apparent. He flops. His joints won't hold. He sticks some part of himself in your face and wiggles whatever is closest.

It isn't even the sexuality of the act that's upsetting; he's never shown off his crotch or derriere like every other two-bit lounge act. If anything, what he's flouted has been pansexuality, a kind of I'll-take-it-all.

But even this has been far less devastating than the anarchy of it all. To Jagger, the stage is more than the kind of narrow space used mostly laterally by rockers; it has a dramatic depth to be used choreographically. Jagger's

Rockford, Ill.

act is part mime, part dance. It has less to do with a display of power—for that you have to go to heavy metal rockers—than with manipulation. There's more sinuousness than raw strength in what he does. And from this comes his real impact. With every move he makes, he seems to be daring the audience to... what? Grab him? Move? Dance? Fight back? It really doesn't matter exactly what. He's taunting you to do something.

Jagger's danced back to center stage and suddenly balloons cascade down about our heads, popping all around our ears. It's a pretty ending to the night yet it doesn't completely erase the memory of what Jagger's dance has been all about. Taunting an entire crowd, like taunting an entire generation, has its dangers.

3

Even now the party's going on—somewhere. No one knows how to make it stop.

The Rolling Stones' tour gathered so much momentum over the past three months that its energy continued building long after Mick Jagger thanked the 13,000 people in the crowd here in the early hours of this morning, walked backstage and stopped the music.

The video crew packed up immediately after Friday's seventeen-city cablecast. Later, the stage crew stumbled around, reeling after fifty shows which had taken everyone in a crazy, frenetic zigzag across the map. And all that's left is a question—Why did they *matter* so much to so many people this time?

The accountants will try to sort out what the numbers mean, but this won't be easy and won't tell the true story. Right from the start the meaning of the numbers was elusive. It was as if everyone knew that raw fact and financial statements wouldn't add up to what the Stones in America would add up to. It was first estimated they'd make $20 million. Indeed, to make ends meet everyone except Jagger

Rockford, Ill.

used vans to get around. Mick liked that waiting limo. Then this svelte figure grew. Next it was a chubby $30 million. And more recently, the spokesmen for the band estimated it as a grossly fat $40 million — and that's not counting untold revenues coming in from sales of *Tattoo You*, the album that came out during the tour. Blur the figures along the bottom line this way and you erode show business's value system. And the erosion goes further: Can, for instance, you compare playing to 300 fans in a Worcester, Mass. club with nearly 180,000 in Philadelphia just a few days later? Which was the real warmup? (Philly fans will tell you.) Which more important? (Worcester.)

Was having four million people demand some of the only 100,000 tickets available for the five shows in the New York area more remarkable than the fact this response happened in less than sixty hours and required 125 part-time postal employees to handle it all? Which better indicated the remarkable popularity for a band on the eve of its 20th year?

In October they established a record in San Francisco, packing in 140,000 people for two concerts at Candlestick Park. Two weeks later they set another record when 87,000 fans showed up at the Louisiana Superdome. The two concerts which really mattered most, though, were those in Buffalo and at the Fox Theater, in Atlanta.

In Buffalo, a Canadian concert-by-proxy with 15,000 fans coming down from Toronto, the band and crew alike conceded everything came together for the first time. Here, the tour which had begun in Philadelphia with the same kind of shaky start which had gutted the one in 1978, crystallized around the music, not the name. In Atlanta, later in October, they played what was reportedly their finest set of them all at the 3,933-seat Fox Theater. *Time*, which had apparently seen their vast stadium shows, panned the band, offering "four solid reasons to pass up the rock tour of the year." *Rolling Stone* told its readers that moments such as the small, strictly music Atlanta performance are "what makes the Rolling Stones the Greatest Rock & Roll Band in the World."

Nor did events surrounding the concerts, often a tip-off for the mood of a tour and the

Rockford, Ill.

Buffalo, N.Y.

tone of its reception, in any way give an indication of their steadily growing importance. Shortly after their September rehearsals in the comfortable Long View Farm in Brookline Mass., a scheduled mini-concert in Boston was cancelled. How perfect this could have been—in the old days. Yet no cries of outrage, or of anything, came from either side, pro or con.

In Seattle, during the tour's westward swing, a teenaged girl died after falling fifty feet to her death on the Seattle Kingdom parking lot. Another woman was arrested at the same show after threatening Jagger. Two 16-year-olds were held on different stabbing charges after the Houston concert. A shooting during the second of the three Landover, Maryland concerts resulted in one death and another wounding. Police in Hampton received a bomb threat before the first show.

In 1969, the stabbing to death of a fan at the band's Altamont Speedway concert near San Francisco has been depicted by many pop histories as the event which signalled the end to the explosion of rock in the '60s—and which pointed to the "satanic forces" which

Philadelphia, Pa.

bedevilled the Stones and all those who would follow them.

This time out they seemed beyond the very events they created. There was an unpressured playfulness, even a sweetness, about the band this time out, coming more from their fans than them. It was as if a big brother had come back home safe and just knowing he was there made everyone else feel safe.

It had more to do with aging, than age. As long as they were out there, playing as vitally as they were, all of rock's assorted generations, from the '60s, '70s and, yes, the '50s, could feel the connection of the music with its past. The Stones are that connection, maybe the only around now. With them, it is history as celebration.

I accept a ride from two guys in a van although my hotel's not far from the Hampton Coliseum. Tony and Jon. They're in their late 20s, unmarried, no plans. I can smell dope, although none is offered.

"I wonder what it would've been like to've seen the Beatles?" asks Jon as the van stops and starts through traffic.

Tony says nothing.

I tell them I remembered the great screaming flashbulb popping Beatles' extravaganzas. "You know, they weren't always taken seriously."

"But the Stones were, right?" Tony says, looking hard at me.

"Not always," I say. "Not like this, anyhow."

Typically, what we were talking about was not the band but our feelings *about* the band. The Stones have become a sentiment not yet made sentimental.

And they are, in truth, rather removed from all this. They live in a floating paradise, always in motion, from private jet to stage to hotel suite and back into the jet and the air again. Hermetically sealed away from nearly everyone and everything else by guards, lawyers, technicians, women friends, they live lives of climatically controlled celebrity.

And this won't stop even if this tour is the last as has been rumored time and time again. They can never completely stop being, as Stones, objects of this view. They've gone too far. Keith Richards will play guitar until he drops, the rock'n'roller without a shred of guilt. Ron Wood will tag along. Bill Wyman and Charlie Watts, both of whom stopped being Stones years ago, even if they continued to play with the others, will always be country gentlemen, Wyman in southern France, Watts in Yorkshire.

And Jagger? At the tour's beginning, Phillip Norman, of the *London Sunday Times*, noticed him backstage at Philadelphia and thought that the singer "from a distance, was eerily unchanged." Actually, he has changed. He now looks more like his early pictures than he did back then.

He has become our generation's Duke of Windsor, the perpetual stylist, a man frozen in place by his own history.

Hampton, Va.

New York, N.Y.

4

PHILADELPHIA,
SEPTEMBER 25

Backstage: Jerri Hall's here. She's Mick's girl friend, the model, the golden, smiling Texas girl. Jade, Mick's nine-year-old daughter, is here, too. There's Ahmet Ertegun, the powerful president of Atlantic Records, the band's North American distributer checking out his investment. And there's Bill Graham, whose Fillmore ballrooms in the '60s saw the rise and fall of rock in the '60s. His company, Raindrop Productions, with up to 100 people involved, is handling the staging. Part of his own job is to keep egos in line. "This," he tells me, with that absolutely evil grin of his, "is not just a rock and roll tour. This is the Rolling Stones."

Hmm. I remember he told me the same thing about Janis Joplin fourteen years ago. Graham is rock's Otto von Bismark. He not only always seems to be exactly where rock history is made but, inevitably, he's also in a position of some power. Lots of power. Even so, he's truly excited by what's happening all around him.

Journey doesn't seem to be so excited. Along with Thorogood opening the show, the San Francisco-based band looks glum: they were nearly booed offstage after suggesting —at a Stones' concert yet—they were "America's No. 1 band." Months later, Steve Perry, Journey's singer, would be slightly more philosophical about what happened. But just slightly. "Let's say it was a learning experience to see how the Stones work," he says. "There's a lesson there—they were really enjoying themselves."

While the Stones were comfortably settled in their suites in the Barclay Hotel facing Rittenhouse Square, their fans had been lining up outside John F. Kennedy Stadium since the night before, with sleeping bags, mini-tents and backpacks; fans from all over the Delaware Valley, from New York and Washing-

New York, N.Y.

Denver, Colo.

ton, two couples in from Montreal. Tickets were sold out soon after they went on sale August 27, and they went quickly again after the second show was announced. Everybody knew what to expect—180,000 Stones' freaks, two, three generations, all packed hip to haunch into a football field under a surprisingly hard and hot late September sun. The promoters, a firm called Electric Factory Concerts, were looking at something else, a gross of $2.7 million.

The talk was about tours, as Bill Taylor, a writer for the *Philadelphia Journal,* would note in a piece appearing the morning of the second concert, Saturday: "When the Stones come out from under their rock and hit the touring trail—a phenomenon that happens, regular as clockwork, every three years—what they do is something which transcends mere music. You don't get a concert so much as a rock'n'roll happening, an electrical storm of fevered emotions and jagged—I'm tempted to say Jaggered—nerve ends. People talk about the various tours, '72, '75, '78 and now '81, as milestones. There's no other band I know, not the Who, not Led Zeppelin, not the Grateful Dead, can do this. So maybe the Stones really are the best rock band in the world. It depends on what you judge them on."

The subway station serving the sports complex center has become an enormous amplifier as kid after kid comes off the train with something from *Tattoo You* blaring on their radios.

John Allan, his girl Betty, her girl friend Suze and the couple they'd picked up hitchhiking, Marvin and...did-anyone-get-her-name? ...anyway, they're passing around a joint at the back of John's Chevy. Beers are brought out, despite the presence nearby of Philadelphia's finest.

They're in from Reading, Pennsylvania. John and Betty have been living together for almost a year now, they tell me. Suze just broke up with the guy she was engaged to.

"We've talked about getting married," says John Allan with a glance at Betty. "But we can't afford to. But it's okay this way—

Philadelphia, Pa.

Rockford, Ill.

Detroit, Mich.

Chicago, Ill.

Rockford, Ill.

Rockford, Ill.

Buffalo, N.Y.

unless we want kids, I guess."

The joint's passed around once more, and nothing's said for the moment.

"This is actually our vacation," he goes on. "We were thinking about going camping but we figured this was special and we couldn't pass it up."

More silence. Then a bit more talk. He's a mechanic I find out, and loves it. He spent two years in university and was doing well but realized he'd rather work with his hands. "Besides, I figure it's safer this way, working on cars and trucks, I mean. I can do it anywhere, right? We've been thinking about moving, you know, going west. We've heard a lot of good things about Arizona."

I know I like this tall, broad-shouldered guy with a great droopy mustache and longish hair. Betty's short, hard and thin-lipped. He seems worried, but she seems unhappy. They're in their late 20s.

"I listen to Bruce Springsteen a lot," she says suddenly, bringing the thought in from out of nowhere. "*The River*, you know it?"—I nod—"It's real. Like what they do, the Stones. There's so much bullshit around these days, you need something that's real."

So more beers are opened and we talk about what Stones' albums we like best. It's one of the main topics of conversation here, along with where one can find a cold beer.

Eventually I thank them and start to leave, when Suze tells me, quietly, that Betty's pregnant and they don't know what to do. The concert is their escape.

Fortune plays fast and loose with the Stones, but it's on their side to start their tour. There's a teachers' strike in Philadelphia's School District's seven senior centers, and a huge part of the audience, which might otherwise be occupied, is able to come to an all-afternoon event. As for those kids who were expected to show up at school—well, one Thomas Madell, assistant principal at Plymouth-Whitemarsh High School, thought the band could have chosen a better time, like a weekend. Absenteeism in Philadelphia mysteriously shot up between 10 and 29 percent.

Things are getting out of hand so I start to make notes, like: "Keith Richards was walking around the Barclay's lobby last night with a bottle of Jack Daniels. The hotel staff was not amused. He was."

And: "Jagger turned up early this afternoon to check out the sound equipment. He's being quoted in an interview by Maureen Cleave, that the *Philadelphia Daily News* is running, as saying: 'Rock'n'roll is a spent force in that we can't expect any more from it,

Syracuse, N.Y.

either as music or an instrument for social change. It is merely recycling itself and everything is a rehash of something else. I'm not that good a musician to break out of it; it's all I can do. If I were a jazz musician with a brilliant technique then to go on doing it would be galling. I can't go on leaping around forever—it would be unseemly and perhaps I shouldn't be doing it even now—but I would be stupid not to do it, while I still can. In any case, if I can't hit middle C, I'm not going to cancel; nobody's going to notice.' "

"He was wearing a baseball cap and brown jacket when he checked the sound system."

And: "Police say thirty-two people have been arrested for drugs and related charges.... The $15.75 tickets were being scalped for up to $60 each the night before. By show time scalpers were lucky to get $20. JFK Stadium is *that* big and the entire field is filled in a first-come, first-served basis.... Officials are dishing out facts and figures left and right: there are 350 security guards, they say, and 100 ushers. Remember what Peter Rudge, a sometimes road manager for the Stones, said years ago: 'It's only rock'n'roll but it's expensive.' "

And: "The Stones aren't the only act in town today. Eddie Rabbit, the country-pop singer, Gary U.S. Bonds, and Lene Lovich are all playing Philadelphia tonight and there's a 'John Coltrane Commemorative Concert' at the Water Works Cafe just behind Philadelphia's Art Museum. The Pretenders are here next Wednesday. And Peter Tosh is here Thursday. Whew! Who is Mick Jagger, anyway?"

Thorogood was on before noon. Journey was offstage by 1:45. By the time the Stones

Detroit, Mich.

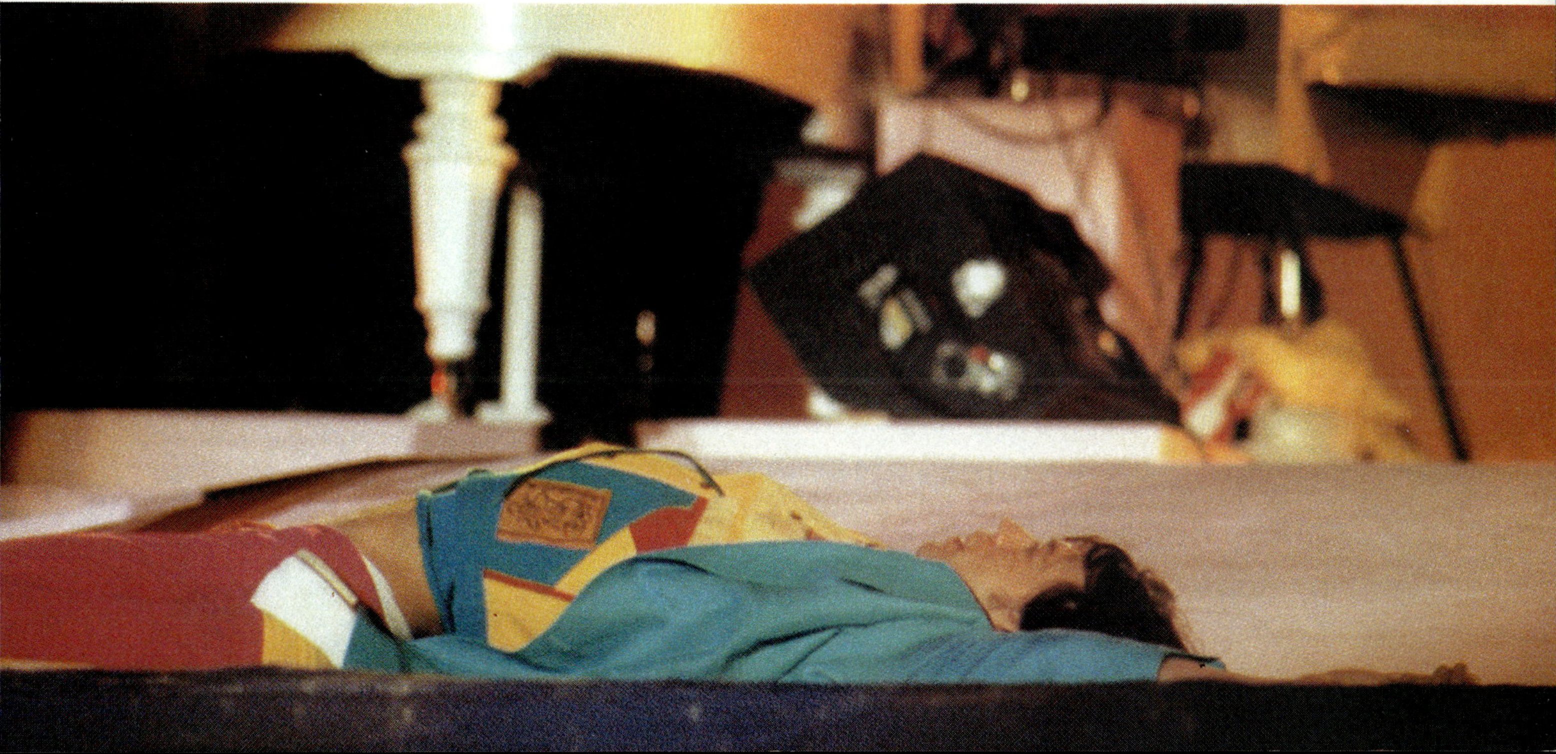

are on—my watch says 4:47 P.M.—the crowd's so worked up it lets out not a cheer as much as one vast roar of relief.

I make my way backstage again, as the band's early songs start bouncing around this vast oval of fake Gothic arches and dull red-colored stone into which 90,000 kids are jammed. Something's not quite right with the music. Something's missing, but I'm not sure what. Faces I see backstage confirm this. Famous local groupies and record company hacks and big-time, small-time and medium-time local deejays are here. Critics have flown in from Los Angeles and London. Everyone's here. And less than an hour into the very

New York, N.Y.

Buffalo, N.Y.

first Stones' show, all these people, workers and hangers-on alike, have come to realize the same thing: *It isn't working*.

The Rolling Stones are bombing in exactly the same city they bombed in at the start of their last tour in 1978.

Chord changes are being missed, words forgotten, and there's no thrust, no energy. Overhead a tiny plane circles pulling a banner with a feminist message complaining about the words to *Under My Thumb*, the very first song, no less.

Some knew it might happen this way. They almost expected it. Immediately before the band started out, friends, workers and just people close to the band whispered that this might well be "the last time."

It all had to do with Jagger. Keith Richards, the guitarist with the skull ring on one hand, the cockeyed smile and every note Chuck Berry ever played deep in his bones, would tour for ever and ever. But not Jagger. Mick Jagger, it was rumored, was having attacks of conscience and it all revolved around one question: Was he too old? This had nothing to do with the physical process of aging: at 38, he was probably in better shape than he was at twenty-eight. He'd stopped smoking, cut back in his drinking, and with Jerri Hall he'd found someone he felt comfortable with. It

Detroit, Mich.

was a question of appearance: "It might appear unseemly," he'd said, "to be out on a rock tour at our ages."

We'd been talking about this long before the tour was announced, although it was being considered. It was in their offices, high over Rockerfeller Center. In one office was Keith, in the other was Mick, and in between was Woody. So much for organization. Over the period of a half hour, Keith announced it was all planned and Mick said *nothing* was planned. "Playing live makes a band, a band," Richards said in the office he was using as he poured a giant shot of Jack Daniels into our glasses. "You not only get to practice what you're doing but you get to feel, right from the body heat, what the people think about it."

But a little later, down the hall, Jagger, in another office, was worried. "We only tour when *I* want to, not before," he said. "I like performing, you know, but there's that question of seeming too old. I know what I used to think of people my age."

Finally, Jagger relented and decided to go out in style, complete with a rented executive Boeing 727, although costs elsewhere were cut wherever they could be. Hence, also, the decision to go out in good shape, musically and physically. They decided to rehearse in isolation—well-appointed isolation, at that, at a studio-cum-residence called Long View Farm, surrounded by good dairy pasture land. The Long View farm, in Brookline, Mass. comes equipped with 24-track studio, pool room and rehearsal rooms; Pat Metheny has used it as has Aerosmith. The Stones practiced nightly there, and Mick jogged up to 12.5 kilometers daily to get himself in concert trim. To get the feel for all the old songs, they were practicing *Jumpin' Jack Flash*, *Brown Sugar*, *Honky Tonk Woman*, *Satisfaction*, and *Just My Imagination*. They decided to do something they had not tried since they appeared at the El Mocambo in Toronto in 1978—they decided they'd play a tiny club nearby, a 300-seat tavern in a blue collar town an hour from Boston.

At the El Mocambo, they'd run into a pack of trouble. First, Keith was arrested by the Royal Canadian Mounted Police for possession of heroin. Margaret Trudeau, then wife of Canadian Prime Minister, Pierre Trudeau, travelled to New York the same time as the band did after she'd turned up unannounced at the club, sparking months of rumors and counter-rumors, at least in Canada.

At Sir Morgan's Cove, the Worcester club, things barely went any smoother. News that the Stones were going to appear there leaked out early enough and, days before the band had actually moved its equipment inside, most newspapers around the country knew that the first Stones' concert would be one they probably couldn't cover. Quickly enough, everyone had uncovered the band's nom-de-group for the occasion: The Cockroaches.

By the time the thirty-foot-long motor home pulled up in front of the club on Green Street, police estimated a crowd of over 4,000 fans was on hand, some laying on car tops, others perched on rooftops, others along sides of walls, and everyone bellowing, "Stones, Stones, Stones..."

The police were not pleased at all this enthusiasm, and by the time the band's two-hour set was finished, had arrested eleven people for an interesting variety of offenses.

All this had contributed to giving the tour a classic—if misleading—overtone. It looked as if the Stones were still rock's bad boys. Riot indeed. And what happened next seemed to confirm this. The band had decided to play another two warmup dates, these in Boston's cozy, 2,800-seat Orpheum Theater. Dozens of kids even waited out in the rain looking for tickets to the gig. But worried about what had happened in Worcester, Boston mayor, Kevin White, blocked the licence for the concerts. Then an open-air site at City Hall Plaza was suggested, but that was rejected by the band.

So there it was—*banned in Boston*. Perfect. A classic hassle-filled Stones' tour was shaping up and with it the idea that rock'n'roll was still alive and kicking up trouble.

But it isn't. In fact, here in Philly it's falling flat until...what? They've begun *Time Is On My Side*, the old Jerry Ragavoy tune they played when they were snotty upstarts on the English rhythm'n'blues scene, making it in London's King's Road joints. And as its bluesy arpeggios roll out into the air, the crowd sings along with Jagger. Amazing: 90,000 kids,

Buffalo, N.Y. →

many not even born when the Stones recorded it eighteen years before, were all being mini-Jaggers.

It's a wonderful moment and it says something about the tour—that it'll be as much about loving the Stones and loving what they're about—and remembering what they were—as it will be about music.

It'll happen somewhere between the present and nostalgia.

Jagger seems stunned—well, at least bemused. And suddenly confident. He looks the way a veteran boxer looks when he realizes he's going to win again but only because of the tricks he knows.

The concert will last two hours and twenty minutes and will run twenty-four songs. He'll sweat and heave buckets of water at those pressed against the fence directly in front and below the stage. It will come to a peak, theatrically, during *Jumpin' Jack Flash*, when he plays the role and is hoisted up above the crowd in a cherry-picker crane to throw carnations down.

But the sentimental heart of it all comes when the crowd responds. In effect, Mick Jagger is leading a sing-a-long.

PHILADELPHIA, SEPTEMBER 26

The second show here has gone the way the first did: sloppy, not always confident but still crowd-pleasing, as Jagger sang *Jumpin' Jack Flash* while being held high above everyone's heads in a cherry-picker crane. Afterwards I've given up trying to find a cab on Broad Street and decide to wait in a nearby corner bar. It's a black bar where middle-aged couples dance in a deep-red neon gloom and the young men drink their beers out near the street curb. There's no tension here, just a profound sadness—time is not on anyone's side in this part of Ronald Reagan's America.

"I was just at the concert," I begin to tell the bartender. The look she gives me indicates she hasn't the slightest idea of—or concern for—what I'm talking about. The Rolling Stones' tour doesn't matter in this part of Philly.

The music does, though, at least if you listen to what's on the jukebox here. As I finish my beer, I catch the crisp disco bass-line by Bill Wyman thumping metallically out of the box to introduce *Miss You*. The middle-aged couples move slowly to their seats as younger couples get up and dance.

Jagger's voice is reduced to pure snarl on this tiny sound system. It's a voice you'd know anywhere. His signature high, always slightly put-on and grating. When he sings of sex no one can touch him. Sex, to Jagger, is its own rebel music.

Outside, again, I head back to my hotel. Stragglers are still making their way on Broad Street into the heart of town and in the gloom I can hear people talking about "them"—the Stones.

Philadelphia, Pa.

Denver, Colo. →

But they've already left for another city.

Movement is almost an illusion on the tour. It gives the appearance of change where there is, in fact, little change. They'll play in nearly identical concrete football stadiums throughout the country in nearly identical suburbs to nearly identical white, middle-class audiences, who'll respond at nearly identical points in the show. Denver might just as well be Detroit.

Mick says when a tour's all over, he forgets about it completely. No wonder.

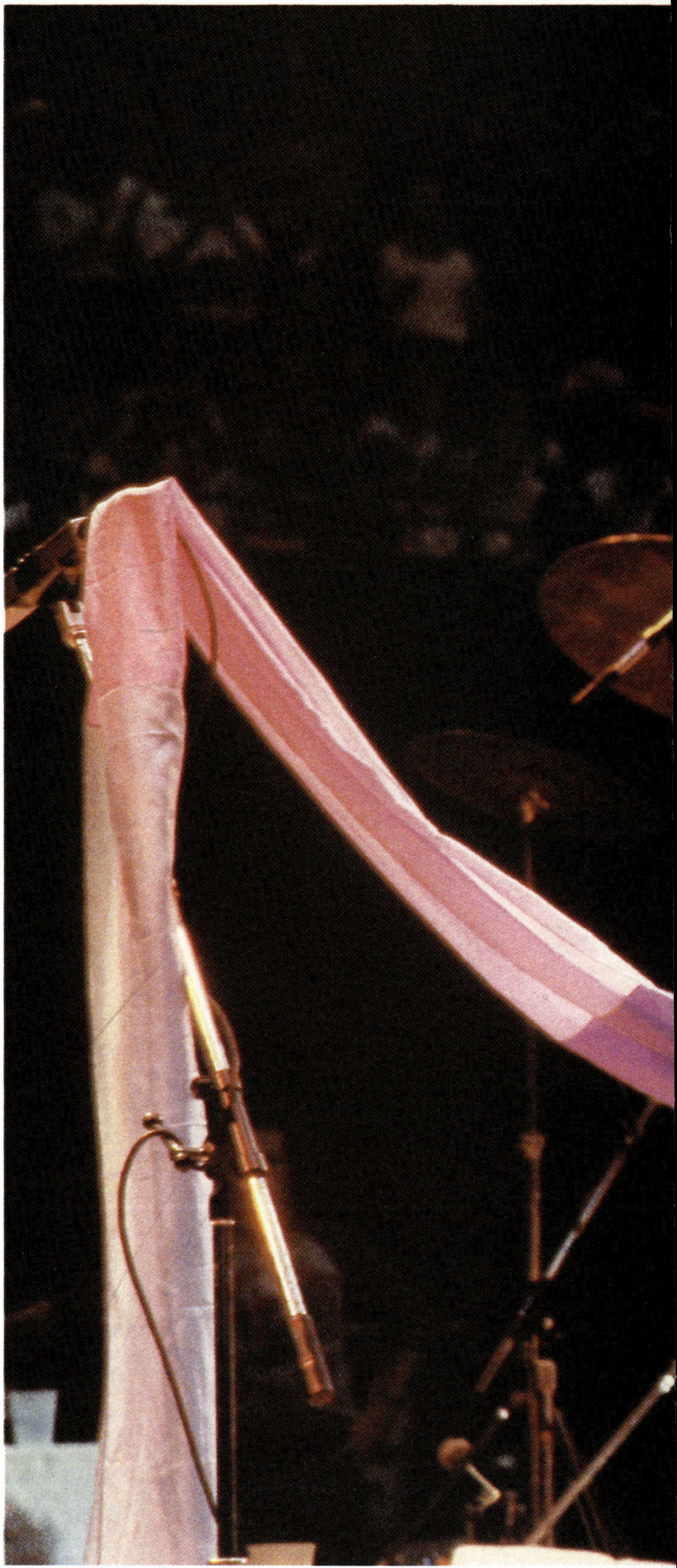

New York, N.Y.

Rockford, Ill.

Detroit, Mich.

Hampton, Va.

Hampton, Va.

Detroit, Mich.

5

BUFFALO, SEPTEMBER 27

The Stones are famous because of Mick Jagger—they're a band because of Keith Richards. And it's here where Richards, in black leather as always, has turned this ragtag crew of greying superstars into a genuine rock'n'roll band.

Here, in a 2½-hour show, the tour begins, musically. Ron Wood swaps darting guitar solos with Keith; Charlie Watts, rock's steadiest drummer, pushes the pulse while Bill Wyman, cradling his bass, merely looks bemused.

It's a fine, dramatic day: hard, driving winds have almost shredded the set with its new-wavish design and its pastel colors. It's also a strategic day. This is as close as they'll come to Canada, and 15,000 of the 75,000 fans here are from Canada, fifty kilometers away. The Stones haven't been fond of Canada since Richards was arrested in Toronto in 1977 and was sentenced to play two concerts for the blind in nearby Oshawa in 1979. But Jagger knows his marketing—there's still all that Canadian money. "It's very nice of you to make the trip," he tells them sweetly. A great, self-congratulatory cheer echoes back.

Denver, Colo.

"The toughest, shrewdest businessman to emerge on the entertainment scene since Bob Hope and Frank Sinatra," is how *Rolling Stone* magazine now describes Jagger. With guidance from the band's financial adviser, Prince Rupert Loewenstein, Mick convinced Jovan Inc., the multimillion dollar perfume company, to sponsor the tour (the company gets rights to print its name on concert tickets: the Stones get about $4 million). Ticket sales were rigidly controlled, as were sales of T-shirts, buttons and badges. "Nothing happens that isn't cleared with Mick," says an insider. "Nothing."

They've dug back into their past for a song from their very first album, *Down The Road Apiece*, and it fits perfectly into the flow of the show. Watts and Wyman push the rhythm to the verge of being too fast. This extra bit of tension works. Jagger grabs a guitar and aims it at the audience for *When The Whip Comes Down*. *Let's Spend The Night Together*, once censored to *Let's Spend* ***Some***

Philadelphia, Pa.

Time *Together* so it could be performed on the Ed Sullivan show, is streamlined too into something sleek and modern, with the rhythms again sped up. It's hot.

Ron Wood is in fine form, skittering from side to side, kibbitzing first with Jagger then with Richards. Onstage, Woody becomes the one true crazy, the only one who seems to be out of control. Offstage, at least in public, he's the opposite. For *Beast Of Burden* everything's and everyone is in place. This is one of the band's great songs, a piece of rock'n'roll that has a similar tone and rich poetic resonance the best songs of The Band had. And they don't throw it away.

The media attention has been intense. Buffalo television stations have posted reporters outside the hotel the band's in and are interviewing porters and just about anything that moves and looks like it might have anything to

Buffalo, N.Y. →

Buffalo, N.Y.

Come to where the flavor is.
Have a Coke and a smile.

O.J. SIMPSON
DISCOVER
PLYMOUTH ROCK
97Rock

Philadelphia, Pa.

do with the Rolling Stones. The Canadian media is here in force, too. Early on it was rumored the band might, indeed, play western Canada ("Just to snub the east which has given them so much hassle," joked a press agent, referring to Keith's arrest). When this notion was scotched, Buffalo became the next best opportunity. One Toronto radio station is doing direct live reports from the stadium, and in between is playing recorded versions of the songs in the order the Stones play them. Buffalo rock radio stations are giving live reports, too, with an added sense of urgency. A tremendous storm had blown up earlier in the day and it looked, briefly, as if the concert might be cancelled. Reports are on air every quarter hour or so reassuring listeners, "It is on, I think I saw them come in."

I'm sitting high up in Rich Stadium directly behind the stage, getting better sound than most of the crowd as well as getting a different view. And I'm watching Richards.

A lot of rock is designed to show off the act; the Stones' act is designed to show off the music, even when Jagger plans to ramble. There's nothing particularly revolutionary in

this, of course. Mozart's operas or most blues have similar intentions. But it's becoming increasingly rare in rock as young and younger acts come along which are further and further removed from what originally motivated the music. Watts and Wyman, the oldest rhythm section in rock, could very well be the best. They're certainly the steadiest, playing with remarkable finesse and remarkable compatibility—just ever so slightly ahead of that exact point where the beat should fall: pulling the pulse along after themselves. But it's fallen to Keith Richards to sculpt this rhythm into meaningful shape. The shape comes with the style and for all of his references to great rhythm guitarists of the '50s, exactly what he sounds like has never been easy to define. The meaning comes from his sensitivity to the words.

He likes to talk and like any true talker he's given to gossip and reminiscence. On the other hand, Mick, for all the interviews he's given and for all he's used to dealing with the media, relies a lot on the interviewer understanding the tone of his conversations. I suspect one reason Jagger came to use his body

Buffalo, N.Y.

Denver, Colo.

Buffalo, N.Y.

so well is that he found it could express things he might not otherwise be able to say verbally. I also suspect that he doesn't always trust words, which is perhaps why he uses them so well in songs.

But his partner is a true believer in words as in other things. "The problem with Keith," a friend of his once told me, "is that he thinks rock'n'roll is real life. In this way, he's the most naive person I know."

We were standing outside of Toronto's Harbour Castle Hilton hotel on a mean February night in 1977, the night after the Stones had played their first club date in years at the El Mocambo just north of the city's garment district up Spadina Avenue, and only a few days after Keith's arrest. The thought that he might end up in jail had brought up the question: Would the Stones ever tour without him? The question should have been, *could* they? In either case the answer was immediately apparent—no.

Detroit, Mich.

He is to the Rolling Stones what they are to the rest of rock—the proof that they connect with whatever vital force out there that got rock going in the first place. In North America, rock was a poor boy's music taken up to the middle class. (In England, it's often functioned in an entirely different and sometimes reverse way, with the working class interpreting other working-class music—The Specials adapting Ska just for one instance—for its own purposes.) Somehow, though, in a North American context, rock works best when it never settles in completely with those adapting it.

By every criteria going the Stones could perhaps be called a middle-class band. Only two of the Stones could be said to have working-class backgrounds—Charlie is a truck driver's son and Bill is the son of a bricklayer. But then there's the jet-setting luster Jagger has given their image. But he can jet-set all he wants—or all we suppose he wants—

New York, N.Y.

Hampton, Va.

Hampton, Va.

Chicago, Ill.

Syracuse, N.Y.

because Keith will connect the band with its music's roots.

"We're always asked what we're going to do when we get too old for rock'n'roll," Keith told me once. "But what can you say? It's the only thing we've done—the only thing I've done. It's the only thing I want to do."

I remember this conversation as I watch him in Buffalo. He doesn't just start a song as much as he wrenches it out of his Telecaster. And it's never exactly the same way twice. The opening chords to *Honky Tonk Woman* are slightly rougher one time, slightly louder the next.

He's so frightfully frail-looking, rail-thin, his face pasty white, almost gaunt. His paleness makes him handsome. Obviously, it's

Philadelphia, Pa.

not the usual things in life which sustain him.

"We never see each other enough these days," I also remember him saying. Again, it was in their New York offices and months away from any live concert—neither situation to his liking. "Mick's always somewhere where I'm not and the rest of the band's scattered around the world. And that's not the best situation to work on your music. I mean, we have to do it by phone.

"Back when we started when we were just scuffling around it was different. We were living together. We'd see each other all the time. I'd start something and bring it to someone else and he—usually Mick—would add something to it.

"We were writing all the time. The music was everything."

NEW YORK, OCTOBER 5

6

"I know this may sound dreadful," Marianne Faithfull is saying, "but Mick is not my class. He's not exactly working class, not poor certainly, and there's only a slight difference between us—but it's there."

The band has found its musical groove and headed west. I've gone east to meet the woman with the throaty voice who was there when they started, who once epitomized swinging London, who knew the Beatles, hung out with Richard Avadon—and who was Mick Jagger's girl friend.

Marianne is here to promote a new album, *Dangerous Acquaintances*, but I want to talk to her for another reason: whatever this Rolling Stones' tour is all about, she represents its opposite meaning. The Stones have turned the '60s into a road show. She's done something else, something certainly as important—she has survived. She's in her mid-30s and is no longer the hip Ophelia with the pale cornstalk hair. Her own albums are survivor's albums: gutsy and sensual. They're also cathartic, as she tries to sort out her own past.

"Me, Mick, everybody, we all believed it, you know," she goes on. "We thought we could change the world. I guess I just believed in it more than most. Fool. None of us could have achieved what we wanted. We were all flying too high. We were trying to get too much, too quickly, too soon." She sounds bruised, but not bitter.

"I always knew I was an artist. I was taking my final exams and was thinking of going to Cambridge—I was also a terrible cultural snob at 17—but the minute Andrew Oldham, the Stones' producer, you know, the minute he said, 'come to London and make a record,' I went. And I was right to do it. I didn't make any money from it, but I was right not to lock myself into Cambridge."

She swivels around in her chair; she's sitting cross-legged to watch a dry, opaque pale yellow sun set over the city. Years before she'd been living in a cheap London flat

New York, N.Y.

Buffalo, N.Y.

Syracuse, N.Y.

watching TV with a few friends one night, when Tony Richardson's 1969 production of *Hamlet* with Nicol Williamson was aired. And there she was, too, hair lustrous and long, with full, pouty lips—the mod as pre-Raphaelite British Beauty. An Ophelia of the '60s.

"It staggered me," she remembers. "I didn't know.... I just didn't realize how *beautiful* I'd been. I wept. I suddenly saw this little creature I'd been and I saw that incredible luminous quality that was there."

Her hair is shorter now and her breasts are fuller and threaten to pop a button on the lacy Victorianesque blouse she's wearing. And

Rockford, Ill.

she is, to me, far more beautiful now than even the most "atmospheric" pictures had once showed her to be.

She has a toothache, but it won't stop her from reviewing her role in the '60s with—and without—the Stones: replaying them back and forth, like a director looking at old footage trying to decide which scenes to keep and which to cut. She was, after all, in one of the most famous scenes from the '60s—the "young woman" found by police at a Rolling Stones' party nude under a "tawny fur rug," in one of the more famous arrests in the '60s when both Mick and Keith were charged. An editorial in *The Times* of London, no less, came to their support, but by then she'd become the token Mod scarlet woman. Mick went on national television to defend their living together. The Archbishop of Canterbury denounced her from his pulpit.

"I used to get letters, letters that were so wicked," she says, "ones that would say, 'You contaminate this country and the sooner you

Detroit, Mich.

Buffalo, N.Y.

and your long blonde hair float out to sea the better.' "

She reaches for a cigarette and says something quite remarkable: "But I've always known I was on the side of angels. I know I am. I am not guilty. I'm beginning to think that what happened to me, to us all, Mick, everyone, was something very English. Was it I betrayed my class running off with Mick? You know that's what is so sick about England, these little degrees between people. But they're there. Joe, Mick's dad, who's really great, is a teacher. My mother was a teacher as well; that was how she earned her living after she split up with my father whom I really didn't know very well. But my father was a professor and my mother was also a baroness. But because I looked like an angel and did all that I did, it was if I'd committed some frightful crime."

Detroit, Mich.

She looks back at the sun for the moment. Her first marriage to John Dunbar, a writer and scholar who, she has said, reminded her of her father, broke up after she started living with Mick and the roller coaster of her life with drugs and rock'n'roll began. She collapsed in Australia in 1969 and was hospitalized, with Mick at her side—who soon left again. "One of the best things about my relationship with Mick was that it proved that two people from two very different backgrounds could get along very easily. People are beginning to realize that my life didn't stop when I split up with Mick. In fact, it started."

Mick Jagger tells this story:

"So I was in a restaurant one night, a nice one in New York and there was a family at the next table. No one was paying any attention to anyone else but then I heard—I couldn't

21

help it—the kid ask his father something. He wanted to know which band was better, the Beatles or the Rolling Stones. 'Well, I don't know,' says the father. 'Why don't you ask him?' meaning me. It made me feel like something out of history."

He winces. Like a priest who must always entertain the unsavory subject of sin as a part of his life, the lead singer of the Rolling Stones, a millionaire with a diamond in a tooth and with houses in Paris and New York—perhaps the most famous singer of his generation and certainly the most photographed—has to answer to his age.

And answer and answer. Age was an issue before the tour of course, and it loomed larger after it was finished: Why still is the dominant performer in rock a 38-year-old Englishman who has a daughter old enough to be a fan, who stands five-feet-ten, has a head that's large for his compact body, and a broad mouth? Why, at tour's end, did older seem better? For the record: He was born in Dartford, Kent, July 26, 1943, one of Eva and Joe Jagger's two sons. He was thought a bright child who worked hard at school. Through the influence of his father, an instructor in physical education, he ran a lot, was good at sports and took care of himself. He and his brother Chris were friends. He was about as content with his life as a young man of middle-class circumstances could be.

And if he'd followed an early inclination and had, after leaving the London School of Economics, gone into business, likely he'd still be thought of as a young man, no doubt one on his way up. But he took a liking to what his father called "jungle music," and that led to his present predicament, which is this—is it seemly to be a rock'n'roll musician as one approaches forty? Is rock just a young man's game after you've spent over twenty years at it?

The key word here, at least for Jagger, is "seemly." He is not a snob, per se. But he knows what's appropriate and what's not. He knows how ridiculous one might appear trying what he does onstage if the leaps and jeers do not work.

He has a remarkable sense of proportion, of where things should be in the balance. He has been rock's ultimate insider, the one who

Rockford, Ill.

← Buffalo, N.Y.

lived next door to John Lennon in New York and sent the reclusive ex-Beatle post cards. But he's also been an outsider, watching it, studying it, profiting by it. He'll admit he's been tempted to go with it completely, to really let loose, but he's never done so.

Through the later '60s everything about him spun crazily out of control: he was sentenced for drug possession; two girl friends, Chrissie Shrimpton, then Marianne Faithfull, tried to commit suicide; his co-star in the movie "Performance," James Fox, soon found religion; Brian Jones drowned in a pool; and it was rumored that he was in league with dark forces of sundry kinds. Yet at the center of it, he was in control. He stayed detached from it, somehow. Deliberately. He played the outlaw in Tony Richardson's movie, "Ned Kelly"; and was criticized for not being tough and hard enough.

One scene from another film, the documentary of the band's concert at the Altamont Speedway, near San Francisco in 1969, tells a lot. We've just seen shots of the melee in front of the stage, with the Hell's Angels mixing it up with the crowd and a young man being stabbed, and there, on the screen, is Jagger. He himself watches the scene. Jagger-watching-Jagger.

Even now. He was offered a bit in the movie version of Broadway's "Annie," but turned it down sensing the movie might be a flop. He walked away from the set of Werner Herzog's "Fitzcarraldo," shown recently in Cannes, feeling that the actual shoot was getting too dangerous. He may act again, but now he's planning to produce Gore Vidal's *Kalki*. He is thinking of doing his autobiography, but is looking for the right ghost writer.

In this way, he is the true hedonist ("Of all

New York, N.Y.

Detroit, Mich.

this, the beginning and the greatest good, is prudence."—Epicurus). Such is his narcissism, it was said, that he married his own image—the pouty Bianca Perez Morena de Macias. Such is his complexity that, since their divorce, he thinks he may never marry again, even though Texas model Jerri Hall is a constant companion these days.

Rock's most famous satyr tends to be monogamous. His taste for travel or his appetite for excellent food and fine wine have certainly not been impaired by being a Rolling Stone, having become a rolling conglomerate with its fish processing plant in Japan among other holdings. But these tastes began long before when he was living with his family. I once asked him if he felt his love of luxury impaired his reputation as a rocker: "You go to St. Tropez, after all; isn't it difficult, intellectually, to do that and feel the urgency of a rock song?"

"Not at all," he said, cutting my idea off at

its weak knees. "You must understand that I was in St. Tropez as a boy. My parents used to take me there."

Shortly before the J. Geils Band was to go out and join the Stones for the European segment of the tour, I talked to the lead singer, Peter Wolf, about age and rock'n'roll. It's no small question, as two distinct and increasingly separate generations are exercising their influence in the music. "All this worry about rock'n'roll disappearing as everyone gets older is just a bourgeoise white hang-up," he said. "You don't see black people worrying that a singer like Bobby Bland is older. Or Ella Fitzgerald, or Sarah Vaughan or Count Basie. No, rock's going to be

New York, N.Y.

Detroit, Mich.

around. It's too important."

But Jagger can't be—or won't be—as blunt about it. It's not a class question with him but a personal one. It's not a question of physicality, but of intellect. As for the physical side of things, he is in better shape for this tour than he'd been in for years. He jogged miles through Massachusetts back roads. He hasn't smoked in years and gargles with glycerine for his voice. He's cut back in his drinking. He's primed and ready, but for what exactly? More and more his music is reaching an audience that's less and less sophisticated than he is. He won't write down to this audience. He believes that *how* something is said in a rock song can be as important as what's said, in a literal sense. But he doesn't believe that because the words are only one part of the texture they don't matter.

The younger generation of musicians perplexes him: "I don't feel connected with bands like The Clash, the bands that still play every night. I can only see them as repeats of everything that happened before. I think it's a bit unfortunate, too, but I think no one would disagree with me. Most musicians in fact do agree with me. Bands like The Selector and The Specials, which are good bands, are repeats too. I mean, I saw bands like that in 1959. It's the same old thing done slightly differently. I like some of the shows that I've seen. I liked the Pink Floyd show—better, anyway, than Elvis Costello's. But I haven't been interested in rock in years—I mean, interested in it in the way of wanting to talk about it. It's not really the 100 percent of everything I'm interested in. I guess, I never have been."

We'd been talking before the tour had begun—before it really loomed over his head and he was forced into his rock'n'roll frame of mind. At least this is how I explained to myself his squinty-eyed view of rock. Later, though, I checked some notes from talks we'd had several years before and there it was again—Jagger circling around the subject of rock and his participation in it.

The notes read:

N.Y. October 6, '77. Mick and Keith sitting together. Strange—they're both in the middle of the couch, not at either end. Their knees are almost touching. They talk about the early days. "We haven't lived together on the road since 1966," says Mick.

"We were living together in London at the same time, right?" Keith reminds him.

"Yeah," says Mick. "That helps, being close together. Over a couple of weeks we'd come up with three or four or five good songs. You see, we didn't have many distractions back then, no girl friends. So if I had a half-finished song, I'd bring it to Keith and he'd finish it. It all worked out rather well. We were both very critical about our songs."

Keith: "That's why *Exile on Main Street* was a double album. We'd been together for a period of time (from 1971 through 1972) and we were writing songs at such a rate we had too many to make just a single album."

Jagger: "Of course, you can't expect people—expect the Stones—to keep living together, to be like they were for always. We still write, of course. I find writing ballads easier when I'm alone because all I have to do is go over to the piano and play them over. With rock songs it's more difficult. I can't build up the enthusiasm, the feeling for the music."

Mick's interest in history has had a lot to do with the music. Especially history of a kind—the blues. "Even when we started playing

Denver, Colo.

Buffalo, N.Y.

ballrooms we played a lot of blues because we didn't know what else to play," he tells a Toronto-based radio documentary team which has followed the tour to Europe. "We'd come from blues clubs to these ballrooms where there'd be bands playing popular tunes of the day. These bands would be dressed up in uniforms, you know, with little red blazers, playing whatever was the hit record of the week. So we very quickly had to evolve so we started doing ballads. We'd always liked them, anyway. It was just that we didn't think we should do them because they are blues. There were always arguments about how many ballads we should do and I never thought we should do that many ballads.

"At the moment I see myself as a functioning rock singer but that's really an old way of looking at it because I can't take it seriously. At the beginning we were a serious blues band alright but I can't really be serious about

Syracuse, N.Y.

what we do onstage anymore because they are such big shows. And because it's been twenty years you can dip into the oldies. It's not like when you were young and you did all the songs you had and you played them for all you're worth. It's very odd when you've got a lot of material to choose from. It's still a lot of fun, but it doesn't seem as intense as it used to be, at least to me. And the audiences aren't as intense. They aren't old fogies sitting there with handbags. There was one horrible period when we got quite old people *only*. Now they're really young but it's still just very good-timey. There's no intensity in it. I'm sure the young people see us as some sort of curiosity. Even if it's AC/DC, it's not intense like it used to be. I guess it's just the period. Who knows? It goes like that in stages. In 1967 in England it was pretty intense."

It was intense for the band on the two nights they ended the American tour, in Virginia in December. Keith and Woody were nervous, for this was going to be on live television: the show was taped for cable TV and would be seen by an estimated 800,000 people in seventeen American cities. Keith was pacing around wondering what they'd got themselves into. Everybody was blaming everyone else. The pressures on him were considerable, because to sing in tune properly he felt he couldn't "fool around" on the stage quite so much. Still, Mick responds well under pressure—it's a condition he's come to understand. And the two concerts went well musically, with a number of tracks on *Still Life*, the live album recorded during the tour, coming from them.

And the show itself worked out well although Mick says that the band didn't make much money from it, "it was expensive to do."

Denver, Colo. →

22

Hampton, Va.

The Rolling Stones work well on television, though. "This band broke out on television," he says. "If it hadn't been for television and shows like 'Ready, Steady Go'...well, it would've taken the band much longer to get where it was going if the band hadn't been so good at TV. I think this band grasped the television style in a way in those early days."

The American critic who suggested about the song *Satisfaction*, that its "lyrics denied what the music delivered," describes what I sense is Jagger's role within the Stones. If Richards is at its heart, he's at its head. He's the Mr. Outside to Richards's Mr. Inside. Jagger is both a part of the group and apart from it. He watches it. He knows it. Everyone goes to Bill Wyman for the facts. But Mick says there's different sets of facts, adding that Bill's history of the band "is only Bill's opinion" of the band's history. "But isn't that what's important? Not the facts but the opinion?"

He doesn't like to be pinned down by facts and says he's upset by all the misinformation about how much money they're said to have made on this tour. No one asked him he points out. Besides, they're not sure themselves.

No wonder he's so physical onstage: he's on the move emotionally, too. He is said to have master-minded the tour, but he shrugs it off, saying in planning for it he merely figured what was spent last time out in 1978 and upped estimated costs 15 percent. So much for master-minding. "It was the biggest tour we ever did—the biggest for anybody. We spent money on it. A lot of people will say to you, 'Why bother spending months on it? Why

Hampton, Va.

Hampton, Va.

not get on and just do it? It's only rock and roll. Get on and do it.' But I think with the money and the time and the effort you spend on the staging that people will want to come back and see it. You could do it much simpler and a lot of people wouldn't care. I know a lot of the band wouldn't care."

"He likes the present, not the past," says a friend who's watched him over the tour. "He'd rather talk about what he or the band are doing now, not what it did long before."

"He's absolutely dead sure of everything he does," says another.

"He wings it. He makes everything up as he goes along," says one more.

His is not a personality juggling contradictions, a pragmatist who's forced by reputation to seem like a dreamer. He knows himself completely. He functions, I think, rather like

Detroit, Mich.

Syracuse, N.Y.

those great athletes who know the game they play so well—who can see it in its entirety and not just what they're doing—that they know what others are going to do in relation to their own moves.

You watch the player follow the pattern for a while, a footballer setting up a pass, then, without noticeable change of pace, he's going entirely against the flow of play, anticipating precisely where it's going to go.

It's an outsider's way of playing the game.

Denver, Colo.

New York, N.Y.

7

SEATTLE, OCTOBER 15

Pamela Lynn Melville, 16, died of multiple head injuries from a 22-meter fall from a ramp leading into the huge Kingdom Stadium onto the parking lot below. The story makes its way into many newspapers, as editors are waiting for a scandal. Another woman is arrested in Seattle for threatening Jagger. But both stories leave a hollow echo. In 1969 a young black was stabbed at the Altamont Speedway, near San Francisco, as Jagger sang *Sympathy For The Devil*, and it was seen as the end-of-an-era. It was *Altamont*, the dark side of Woodstock. This time around the band is seen for what it is—big business with guitars, everywhere setting attendance records in San Francisco (140,000 for two shows) and New Orleans (87,000 for one show). Before the Hartford, Connecticut concert, fans and cops fight and fifty-six are arrested. And elsewhere there is a rape, one shooting death and many arrests at concerts.

Yet, no one thinks the Stones are in any way involved.

ATLANTA, OCTOBER 26

The tour's smallest show is at the Fox Theater—seating capacity for 3,933 people—and, according to many, the best. They're so good in fact that they prompt Robert Palmer, the intelligent and generally cautious rock critic for *The New York Times*, to call them "the Greatest Rock'N'Roll Band in the World."

Rockford, Ill.

Chicago, Ill.

NEW YORK, NOVEMBER 2
Word has leaked out the band plans to end its tour with what they're calling a "video caper," a live concert filmed for closed-circuit TV à la a heavyweight fight. Director Hal Ashby is already shooting footage for the telecast and the concert movie.

NEW YORK, NOVEMBER 12
Five hundred police are needed to watch crowds flooding into Madison Square Garden. A pair of $40 tickets are sold for $500. Over four million people have applied for the only 100,000 tickets available for five shows in the area and 125 part-time postal workers

Detroit, Mich.

Buffalo, N.Y.

Rockford, Ill.

are needed to handle all the extra mail. The tour reaches its very peak of publicity.

"It was just a hobby. When we first started to get write-ups in papers, and reviews, I started to cut them out and stick them in my scrap-book. My ex-wife started it actually, and I thought it would be great for our kid when he grows up. Anyhow, I just carried it on myself and it got really silly. I found I was using one scrapbook a month. Then it was one a week. Then it was one every four days. And after about twelve of them I gave it up. I just started putting the reviews and the clippings in boxes, then it was in trunks. I would collect posters and programs and stickers and whatever was coming in. People would send photos and I'd

← *Buffalo, N.Y.*

Rockford, Ill.

Detroit, Mich.

Rockford, Ill.

keep letters and documents and so it just built up over the years. It got more and more voluminous."

It's somewhere, sometime during the tour, and on the phone Bill Wyman is talking about the history of the Rolling Stones. He's the only one with his own publicist, his own solo hit single (*Je suis un rock star*), and a need to prove he wants to remain a Stone, feeling he was misquoted once in a British newspaper as saying he would be through with the band when he was forty years old.

He's also the band's unofficial historian and has the data and detail of much of the band's past twenty years stored in computer memory banks in his house in the south of France. "The first two years, before anyone knew anything at all about us, were the most important in the band's history," he goes on. He's in a talkative mood, oblivious to pressures which should be affecting him as the tour begins to wind down and winter sets in across America. "That's when the band started writing our own material and we realized what we could do. That's when we started getting all the publicity, which established our image. That's also when we realized that any publicity, even bad publicity, would be good for us. As long as we got our name in the newspapers...

"Every country thinks the Rolling Stones began when we first arrived in that country. So Americans will date the Rolling Stones starting 1964 when they first heard us then. But you see, there's two years missing, two years only avid collectors and real Stones' fanatics know about. In England, they kind of think of the Stones starting in late '63 and in France just after that. In Scandinavia, it's '64. In Australia, it's '65. Yet it was in those first two years when we really stuck by our guns and said we're not wearing uniforms, we're not wearing makeup. We really built the character of the band then. We weren't going to change when the managers, the publicists, and all that arrived.

"It was then when we decided on our approach to things. The Stones are a popular band, a very popular band, because we're not perfect musically. We do make mistakes. We have scruffy endings on live shows and on records sometimes. It makes it seem real.

New York, N.Y.

Denver, Colo.

We've always lived by this rule that if you make a mistake on a recording and if it's too late to change, use it, don't hide it. Don't try to cover it up, wipe it out, lower the volume or fix the mix. Use it as part of what you're doing.

"I think that's what limited disco, for instance. It became so mechanical, all that bounce-bounce-bounce all the time. Every record was the same and I think people like mistakes. They like slight goofs in the Beach Boys, say, when someone sings a bit off-key, or somewhere else when someone drops a drum stick or a bass player hits the wrong note. People remember those things as part of the record. People remember it as being human. That's why people like us, I think. It's our earthiness and street-level kind of appeal we have. It's not intentional, it's just the way we are. We're not super, super brilliant, incredible, technically terrific musicians. Musically, we're just good players who happened to hit on a style. We feel when we play together we play something people find very hard to imitate."

Chicago, Ill.

Denver, Colo.

At a rehearsal before the Oshawa, Ontario concerts in April, 1979, I watched them put together a set. It was in a movie soundstage in the west end of the city and had become an all-night celebrity outing: wives, girl friends and even John Belushi watched as Charlie sat down at his small drum kit to wait until the others decided what they were going to do.

Denver, Colo. →

Detroit, Mich.

Beast Of Burden, Miss You—some songs were run through, some left dangling in pieces, and everything seemed haphazard. One factor seemed to cement things, though—a genuine fondness for how each other sounded. Keith would play something and Mick, or Woody or Charlie or heavens, even Bill, would smile. At one point Mick had begun tickling Charlie, forcing him of his stool.

On the way over, their limo driver told me, they'd been singing *Ninety-Nine Bottles of Beer on the Wall* and other old drinking songs. "It was pretty weird," he said.

To understand the Stones is not to understand what happened in rock'n'roll over twenty years but what happened *despite* rock'n'roll—despite the vicissitudes of commercial radio, fads and flippancies. The Beatles began in the very heart of commercial radio, with Motown, Buddy Holly and the Everly Brothers, and stayed there. The Stones began with the blues, no more fashionable then than

Hampton, Va.

Rockford, Ill.

it is now. From nearly the very start of their careers, the Beatles established themselves as the reasonable and acceptable version of the new order. Not the Stones. They pulled into a petrol station in West Ham, were refused use of the lavatory, and several promptly urinated on a wall—and the story became one further example of renegade rock on the loose.

Stones' fans coming to school with great shaggy mops of hair were told to go home and not come back until their hair was at least as neat as the Beatles'. Very early on then, at least in popular opinion, the polarity had been established—Beatles/Stones, good boys/bad boys, the neat and the mussed. Whatever successes the Stones had—and they started arriving quickly enough—were done upstream and in the wake of that lean, perfectly outfitted luxury cruise the Beatles were steaming ahead with.

It was to be expected from most bands, the Stones included, to react in some way to the Fab Four. But through the Stones another dynamic was established and it was one which proved to be long-lasting. At its most

Buffalo, N.Y.

Denver, Colo.

obvious, it indicated a reaction away from the Beatles, to answer *Let It Be* with *Let It Bleed*. Closer to the point, the reaction was away from the drift rock was taking. Within rock's revolution, so-called, the Stones were staging a counter-revolution even as they marched along with the revolution itself. They weren't alone, of course, nor the most directed in this: Frank Zappa, The Doors, Iggy Pop, the MC5, Captain Beefheart, Grateful Dead, and John Lennon in their own ways were snapping at the hand feeding them.

But as it has turned out, at least when viewed from the context of the last tour, the Stones were the most effective. They're still doing it. On this tour the gap between the new and old songs, between *Start Me Up* and *Satisfaction*, is only that artificial one established by histories. It's not one that's musical. The pieces sound as if they came from the same session. Both the old and the new run contrary to what rock was then and is now. The counter-revolution continues.

The second time Mick saw Keith, the latter had a copy of Chuck Berry's *Back In the U.S.A.* under his arm. Or so the story goes. Nonetheless, the connection was made through the blues. Chuck Berry was just a start. There was Willie Dixon, Bo Diddley, Muddy Waters—they got their name from one of his tunes, *The Rolling Stone Blues*—and Elmore James. But being a blues band was not quite the same thing as being a band that played the blues. The Beatles played some blues. The Dave Clark Five played some blues. Everybody played some blues in those days, but not many did with the ferocity of the Stones.

There was a certain amount of snobbery in their souls right from the start, a kind of reverse-elitism which focused more on the matter of the music's spirit than on its technical, outer matters—and which maintained the band through the end of its first decade when the politics of rock, stemming from their disastrous Altamont concert, turned against them.

Keith's father was an electrical engineer, Mick's lectured in Phys. Ed., Charlie's drove lorry and Bill's was a bricklayer. Taken together, they weren't a working-class band nor a middle-class band—nor were they one

SYRACUSE

that was classless, exactly. They were somewhere in between, growing older in an England that was itself in between its own isolated past and a new, modern Europe. They were suburban.

And then there was Brian Jones, whose father was an engineer. Musically, he was perhaps the most gifted of them all. Mercurial, brilliant, unstable, he tugged them farther and farther in new directions. Keith still wonders at his ability to play almost anything he put his hands on. Bill, too. "Brian was the first person in England to play bottleneck guitar and nobody knew what it was," he remembers. And after his death in 1969, from drowning and drugs and the sheer weight of being a Rolling Stone, the band sprung back to what it was. They probably wouldn't have survived the '60s without him; they may not have survived the '70s with him.

Rockford, Ill.

Syracuse, N.Y.

Philadelphia, Pa.

Denver, Colo.

In one sense, Brian was an outsider in a group of outsiders. No one fit into the Stones —whatever being a Stone meant, then or now. The Beatles, in contrast, seemed to develop a dynamic that was acted out on-stage as well as in the music. There was Lennon versus McCartney, Ringo for ballast, sweetness and simplicity, and George to take them on flights of fancy. Brian grew up near the Welsh border and the rest saw themselves as Londoners. Charlie played jazz. Bill was married. Keith was constantly getting kicked out of school while Mick was not just a student at the London School of Economics, but a *serious* student, with a government grant and all. This could be a group, let alone a band?

Mick was singing with Alexis Korner's Blues Incorporated part-time when the British Broadcasting Corporation arrived one day saying it wanted the band for a radio show. The BBC also said it thought the skinny LSE student wasn't a good enough singer and Long John Baldry got the gig instead. Mick ended up with Keith and Brian in a substitute blues band. Along with bassist Dick Taylor, who ended up as guitarist for Pretty Things, and pianist Ian Stewart—still the unofficial sixth Stone—rehearsals began in earnest. Then Bill Wyman joined in—his job at a store was in jeopardy, anyway. The manager kept complaining his hair was too long. Finally Charlie, who was working full-time as a commercial artist, decided to drum with the band.

It was about this time events started catching up to the band—and they started making good copy. There was the time Mick Jagger supposedly bit off the tip of his tongue during an exercise in gym class. Whatever the singer he was before the accident, everyone insisted he sang much differently after it.

It was also about this time that the flashy publicist who'd hustled The Beatles' *Please, Please Me* for Brian Epstein came into the picture. For a while it was rumored that this hotshot, Andrew Loog Oldham, *was* the Rol-

Buffalo, N.Y.

ling Stones, that they were his complete creation, their long hair, their attitudes, their sound.

They'd just begun to get jobs when Oldham starting showing up. "We weren't a pop band, we just got together and played the blues music we liked to play," Bill is remembering. "And if we could play in front of a few people who liked it—well, that was the ultimate at that time. So we'd do fifteen minutes in small blues clubs with only twenty-three or eight people and it didn't matter to us.

Hampton, Va.

We didn't even face the audience. We used to take stools with us, these old rusty metal stools, and we'd sit on these and never face the audience, let alone play to it. We used to form ourselves in a ring and play to ourselves. Mick would stand there and sing a bit and not move very much. We used to drink beer and smoke cigarettes and not really care. During the interval people would come up and have a beer and say, 'I like that song' and you'd feel kind of good about it. We used the harmonica a lot back then—in a different way than the Beatles did on *Love Me Do*—and maracas, tambourines and that Bo Diddley jungle rhythm format.

"We tried to get that really earthy thing because we liked it. We liked the reality of it. It wasn't fake. It wasn't pseudo. It was really down to earth and very, very exciting. We'd play this stuff to peoples' faces and we'd see their mouths gape. They'd never heard the original records, you see, especially when the kids we'd play for in small places like Peterborough or Luton or Guildford or some place outside of Birmingham. But it wasn't only that they didn't know many of the songs, they didn't know how to dance to the music because the rhythms were quite different. They couldn't sing along or even clap. It was a shock.

"What happened after this was remarkable. In a period of six months, instead of hanging around some horrible club in Ealing or somewhere playing for yourselves and six other people on really snowy nights, we ended up playing to crowds, lines of 500 or 600 queueing up at some big pub in Guildford.

"We'd all had pretty rough upbringings, never too much money, so we never missed having money much. But we did have something to sing about. It was very easy to relate to the music in the early '60s. And you always wanted the real thing. You wanted the Coaster's records to be on the charts, not imitations of them."

Detroit, Mich.

Mick, reminiscing just before the band arrived in Europe for that segment of the tour, to a radio documentary team from Toronto: "We were a blues band, serious, very serious. When we discussed it, we were like students. You know how students get serious about things? It was almost like a theological dispute with us. Mostly it was really imaginary and we were just goofing-off, as they say."

Bill: "It started like a hobby, you know. Brian and Keith in particular, just used to stay in bed all day. They didn't work and there never was any heating in their apartment which was an awful apartment. There wasn't a chair that had four legs on it. All the chairs had three legs and they were leaning against walls and if you tried to sit down anywhere you fell over. There was rubbish everywhere. Mick was still going to the school of economics, Charlie was a graphic designer, doing it in his spare time. Ian Stewart, who plays piano, was at a chemical company and used to cycle to work to save money. He'd prop his bicycle up against the piano in a pub. I'd been married about three years and was earning about twenty to twenty-five dollars a week and was just trying to add a few pounds to my income. Tax free, of course. I used to sit in with a drummer and a local piano player at a social club of sorts. It was very working class and you'd have to play all those terrible songs because people requested them. And that was some more money each week. I had another band in South London and I was earning three or four pounds more a week, so in joining the Rolling Stones I was hoping to

Chicago, Ill.

Rockford, Ill. →

Buffalo, N.Y.

make just a few more bob on the side. It was being paid for something you wanted to do, just several pounds each week.

"But then . . . then it was ten pounds, then twenty . . . and then it was fifty. You know, it got really silly. But we knew who we were. By the time Oldham had arrived we were already 'it', whatever 'it' was. What he did was make it more obvious to the press and public what we were; that we had shaggy hair, that we did not wear uniforms.

"I've got all the press clippings. There were stories that made it seem as if you could see the fleas jumping off our heads. And I was very offended by it and Brian even more so — he used to get really carried away because he could never really deal with it.

"It was really amusing in its way, though. The people we horrified were people we didn't like anyway — the really boring sort of middle-class disc jockeys and TV hosts in England who weren't into it anyway."

Just as it's impossible to determine exactly that point when a piece of blues stops being blues and becomes rock'n'roll, it's unclear when exactly the Rolling Stones ceased being a blues band, per se, and started playing Rolling Stones' music. Late in 1966 a music magazine poll defined them as a rhythm 'n'blues band, the best in the country as the voting turned out with *Satisfaction* named as the top song. But that reflected the year past. Along the way the balances had been tipped. One thing's fairly certain: by the release of *Aftermath* in June of 1966, the process was complete and they were on their own. On the way to *Aftermath*, with the release of some of their greatest early singles — *It's All Over Now*, *Time Is On My Side*, both in 1964, and *(I Can't Get No) Satisfaction*, 1965 — the blues format was still being used if in varying degrees. With *Aftermath*, the blues became the chair, to alter slightly something John Lennon once said, on which the Stones' music sat.

It was as if they'd scooped out something whole and essential from blues for their exclusive use. It had to do with power, but it had much more to do with sex. *Going Home*, the final song on *Aftermath*'s second side, is the mirror image of *Satisfaction*, the finding of release. Stylistically, the piece recalls Delta blues; a filigree of guitar work brought to earth by a great thump of a beat. But this is the frame, the finest-wrought framework imaginable, around a sexual image that hits with the blunt impact of pornography. The Stones began their career with the celebration of sex which is at the core of so many blues. With *Going Home*, they're now on their own turf and in their own terms are celebrating. It's a piece of music about the effect of music. *Going Home*, one of the longest rock songs of its time, is a sexually-charged piece that intertwines a network of cable-work of impulses where sex and music cross and recross lines. It's the aural equivalent of Mick sticking the mike out between his legs or Jimi Hendrix thrusting his guitar out at a crowd — the performance as orgasm.

Riots, parents' complaints, educator's warnings, hotel cancellations, police supervi sion and some of most absurd kinds of public ity

Philadelphia, Pa.

Buffalo, N.Y.

Buffalo, N.Y.

Chicago, Ill.

Denver, Colo.

surrounded them during their first European and American tours. And sometimes they felt themselves they were, indeed, in touch with dark forces.

Jagger and Richards were given stiff sentences for minor drug offenses; they released *Their Satanic Majesties Request*, a druggy, swirling, richly textured album which shows Brian's musical influence over the rest at its strongest. For all its failures, it is a strangely compelling, even beautiful record, with an almost terrifying forced calm about it—the calm before the storm. The Stones' responsiveness to what was around them may have hampered them musically for a while, what with their music seeming to respond to what the Beatles were doing. But 1968 was the year of the revolution—the one that almost hap-

Syracuse, N.Y.

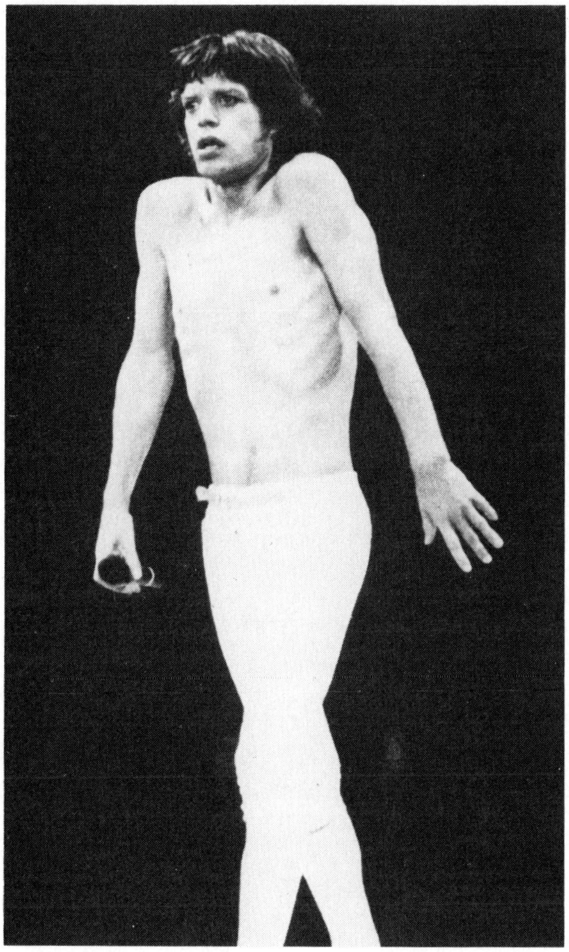

Rockford, Ill.

million people drifted into Hyde Park in London for a concert and his wake, led by the Stones themselves. Jagger read Shelley and a cloud of butterflies was released.

The rhythm of their lives picked up speed. Mick was off to Australia to film "Ned Kelly" and the band prepared for its American tour which followed on the heels of the release of *Honky Tonk Woman*, this the first of a new kind of Rolling Stones song. It had the scope of an anthem, one with which they could celebrate themselves. The tour itself proved to be an ending of sorts. Altamont, December 6, was, everyone admits, badly put together. And when members of the Hell's Angels stomped one fan to death, Altamont made public what anyone who'd been to any rock concert or had listened to almost any rock album had known all along—that the dream of the '60s, whatever exactly it was supposed to have been, had had no hope.

The reaction to the death and the festival "implications" was enormous, however, and the Stones, Mick in particular, bore the brunt of much of it. For there he was, the sweating

pened in Europe and noticeably didn't happen in the United States. The Stones weren't one of the agents for this near-revolution, as much as a reflection of it. At times their response was direct: they released *Street Fighting Man* early in the year which was summarily banned by some American radio stations, who obviously missed its point—and what the Stones were all about. Its narrator hears that revolution is in the air alright but what, he wonders, can a rock'n'roll singer do about it?

But mostly their response to events happening around them was a deeper one. They were in their own kind of turmoil and by 1969 things were rolling nearly out-of-control. *Beggar's Banquet* was selling, Brian Jones and the rest were feuding, and finally it was announced he'd left the group, replaced by Mick Taylor, who'd been John Mayall's guitarist. Brian died July 3, his body found in the pool of his Sussex house. On July 6, a quarter

Detroit, Mich.

Philadelphia, Pa.

Detroit, Mich.

demonic figure bathed in lurid light in the Maysles brothers' documentary of the tour, "Gimme Shelter," released the following year. The picture confirmed that vague notion that somehow "the forces" he was in touch with were unleashed that night. What was less evident, if more important, were other forces which were at work after Altamont and before the band's next tour in 1972.

Whatever else happened as the '60s ended and the '70s began — the "Age of Paranoia" was one phrase used and, of course, there was the on-going soap opera of Watergate — what happened musically was as far-reaching: rock came in from the heat. It was domesticated despite efforts through the late '70s and early '80s to get it back on the street.

The Stones' return tour in 1972 was anticipated with considerable apprehension: What wacko, strung-out thing would happen? Nothing much as it turned out. The Stones released two of their greatest albums — and two of rock's for that matter — through this period: *Sticky Fingers* and *Exile On Mainstreet*. They were already celebrated for their grandiose bravura piece *Jumpin' Jack*

Flash and were soon to be for *Brown Sugar*. And it seemed that whatever would happen to them, for the best or worst, would come about despite what they did with their music.

They'd become *the* Rolling Stones, rock history on the roll, something beyond reach. The tours of the '70s were jet-set spectaculars. Perhaps they weren't as grandiose in a show business way as what Alice Cooper or Yes were concocting, nor as influential as what David Bowie was doing. And in truth, none had the widespread influence that "Saturday Night Fever," both the movie and the Bee Gees' album, had. The Stones' tours were triumphal just the same. It was as if with battles long past they were receiving from the world their due rewards. Entire floors of hotels became their temporary quarters; they dined out in the best restaurants.

Something else was happening though— Keith Richards was slowly poisoning himself

Buffalo, N.Y.

Philadelphia, Pa.

Chicago, Ill.

with heroin. It was becoming, as he once said, "a tunnel that became increasingly narrow." It was also hemming in the Stones. It may be a coincidence but it was about the time he was forced to kick his habit after his Canadian drug conviction in 1977, that the Stones kicked some new life into their music. The main reason the *Some Girls* album was a hit, Keith maintains, "was that I'd kicked junk. We hadn't been in the studio for some time and everybody, including most of the Stones, were thinking, 'Oh well, Keith has finally ridden himself into the dirt.' We got together for that. We threw ourselves together working in a great studio in Paris. It was just another one of

Denver, Colo.

Rockford, Ill.

those things that it was impossible to put your finger on. But it worked."

Mick Jagger's right, of course. There is no one history of the Rolling Stones possible. There are just opinions of what happened.

Denver, Colo.

Rockford, Ill.

"Over the years it was driven into my head that rock'n'roll musicians are not artists," Bill's telling me on the phone, "that they're ignorant and not too intelligent and they break up hotel rooms and all that. It's this attitude—you know, long hair, dirty clothes, not washing—that was around in the mid-'60s that still hangs over us in a way. But when you started being accepted socially in New York, Paris and London, you do feel better. You do meet a better class of people and you're accepted for what you are.

Chicago, Ill.

"When I meet people in France who've made great strides in their careers I'm often in awe of them. Maybe that happens to us too, though. Once in Los Angeles, I invited Peter O'Toole to come to one of our shows and he was absolutely astounded. He said he'd never seen or experienced any energy or any moment in his life that he'd felt at that concert. He said it was like the entry of the gladiators.

"I had to ask him, 'But don't you feel the same thing knowing you are seen by millions of people, in the movies?'

"'No,' he said, 'you don't get that energy feedback, you don't get that amazing spectacle.' He was astounded by it. But me? I don't always think about it much."

Denver, Colo.

Denver, Colo.

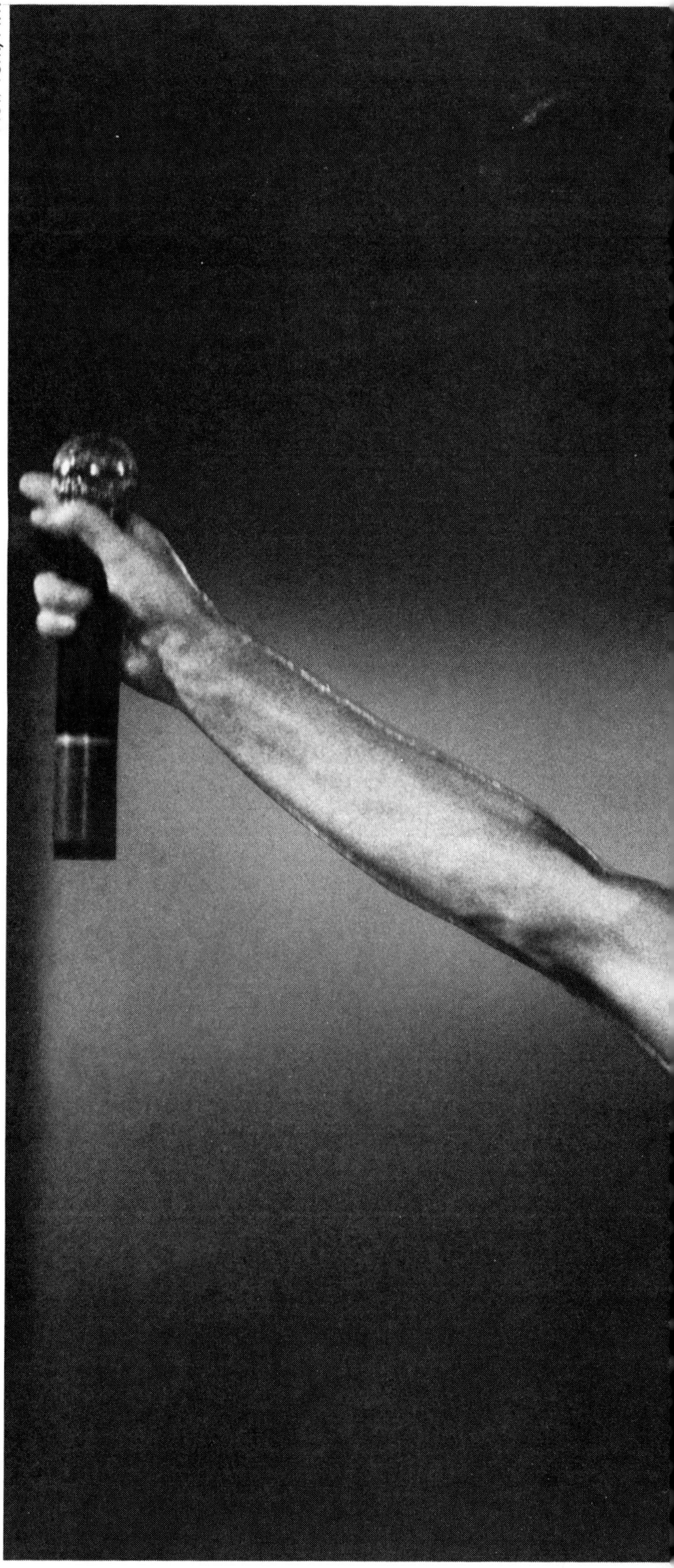

New York, N.Y.

8

MIDSUMMER, 1982

When I started listening to rock it was a private matter. It became a public issue soon enough in the '60s, one with public resonance, but it's back to being a private concern—something which I sense is reflected by the new rock of the late '70s which is in itself more reminiscent of interior "film noir" of the 1940s than anything that preceded it in rock itself. It's the privacy of rock these days, what it means *personally*, to every one of us, that's confusing all of us —at least confusing those who are putting out rock magazines and trying for something that's no longer of broad concern.

I never did figure out a way to explain to my parents what listening to Gene Vincent sing *Be Bop A Lula* meant when I was a kid. It was like talking about sex. Similarly, I can't quite bring myself to tell anyone what listening to rock means to me now, twenty years down the road. I still listen, alright. A lot. New stuff—The Jam, Kevin Coyne or whatever—seems to have some genuine meaning; old stuff—Red Foley, Louis Armstrong and the Hot Seven—do as well; and Duke Ellington, especially him and Count Basie. But it's private, like something I'll tell my wife and no one else. And I suspect I'm not at all alone in my feelings for privacy.

Syracuse, N.Y.

Syracuse, N.Y.

Friends phone and somewhere in the conversation they'll say they just heard such an such an act—more often than not it'll be something totally strange such as The Cramps or Lene Lovich—and that it means a lot to them. I think I know what they're really saying: that they're about to leave a marriage or get into one or change their sexual orientation or forget about sex altogether, or move to the south seas, and that this new (to them) music somehow mirrors this new (to them) feeling. Their attitude is always confessional; they're telling me a secret, something they could never imagine could become public. Let Adult Oriented Rock, or whatever that stuff is called that's on radio these days, drone on and on. It's become just so much electric wallpaper, that constant buzz you hear leaked by Sony Walkmen. Rock itself, the stuff that means anything, has left the mainstream. It's gone inside.

There was one recent exception to this

Chicago, Ill.

though, and that was The Rolling Stones' Tour of America, 1981, and Tour of Europe, 1982. It was the rock's last public gesture, it seemed —public, that is, on that broad scale that rock used to work on.

Other shows, before and since, have attracted a series of large crowds. Top names have landed on the covers of rock magazines. And it all could be called good entertainment, in its way. But it hasn't seemed to matter.

The Stones' tours mattered. The only question is, Why?

I asked Peter Wolf, the J. Geils Band's singer, about this, and after thinking about it for a while he said: "This was the Stones of course,"—he quickly got to one of the nubs of the question. "The economy. For $15 or $20 or whatever it was you could go to this show and get a lot in return. For what you had to pay for, what it offered was a good deal. And in difficult times that means something."

He's right, of course, although another factor should be considered as well. It has to do with generations, two of them in fact: one, the baby boom from the 1940s, the other, the post-baby boom which grew up in the 1970s. Long ago, rock—like all of the instant popular arts—was divided along generational lines.

Now it's come to embrace two generations. To be more precise, it embraces *at least* two generations. One grew up as the music itself did, the other grew up with the music all around it: one with the Stones and the Beatles, the other with their legacies; one in the fractious '60s, the other in the irritated '70s. Both generations—and it's tempting to say, "both

Syracuse, N.Y.

sides" — agree that rock is a good thing. But that's only where the confusion begins, this common agreement, much the way Americans and Canadians remain divided by a common language. Both sides think they agree about the music and its place in the grander scheme of things, but they don't. Both sides think they understand the other better than other generations have understood one another because of a common interest in the music.

They don't.

It's become a question of priorities. For most of the older generation, rock mirrored a concern: brand new emotions and potential revolutions. The next generation has tried to pick up this cue. It's tried to make rock central

Rockford, Ill.

Philadelphia, Pa.

to its life, buying far more records than the first did. Yet all the while it's sensed the music really isn't all that important, that it was there for fun, nothing more or less. Simply put, the second generation needs the sound the way the first needed the words.

Of course, that one style of music should carry such weight over such a broad span of time is remarkable in itself. Those who heard and knew right down in their bones what Elvis Presley was all about, quickly and adamantly rejected what had come before, the big band sound. But the first generation was far less tolerant of the past than the second generation has been. Presley's *Hound Dog* of 1956 came only fifteen years after Glenn Miller (who died in 1944) was at his peak. Yet kids who are now buying Diana Ross's current hits weren't alive when she already a star with the Supremes *twenty years* ago or more. It's possible enough that their *parents* were only teenagers themselves when Frankie Lymon and The Teenagers first recorded this hit, *Why Do Fools Fall In Love*, in 1956.

Throughout the century, popular musical styles have changed every fifteen years or so. In fact, the music industry was banking heavily on some major new force, style or personality to arrive in the early '70s, the fifteen year mark after rock'n'roll first reached the mass, middle-class white market. What the new generation received was not a new kind of

New York, N.Y.

New York, N.Y.

pop, however, but one that was in the scheme of things. Once it supposedly ran counter to the culture all around it. Now it *was* the culture itself; a sense-a-round wrapup of lush sound in Me-places, fern-bars and hair salons and the like. Rock started as a cottage industry: Grace Slick once said The Jefferson Airplane only signed with a big corporation (RCA) in the hope of subverting it from within; the Beatles invested millions in Apple Corp. hoping for a form of western communism. It ended up as a billion-bucks mega-business, outstripping the television and movie industries *combined*. For all of Bob Dylan's cultural clout in the '60s, he once told me that his biggest-selling records "have been in the '70s when everyone was saying I'd gone disco. I just call it Dylan-music."

Although it's no longer the case, rock saturated the '70s, and rock's second generation is giving it a different view of what it was than the first generation has. Take the sense of rock history, itself. To the first generation Jimi

New York, N.Y.

Chicago, Ill.

Hendrix or the Stones were acts they saw or tried to see, they were important, but in a living musical and theatrical sense. But to the second generation, reared on hyped-up rock histories and prepped awestruck deejays or critics who talk reverently about the "greats of the past," Hendrix and the rest are near-mythical figures. The first time I met Janis Joplin, she was slouched in the back of station wagon, suffering from menstrual cramps outside a Holiday Inn in Buffalo. To the second generation, she's almost as great as Bette Midler's "The Rose."

Then again, that rock is seen to have a history at all runs counter to what everyone thought it once was. It was to have been the antidote to such bookish, scholarly stuff, its antithesis. It was meant for the now, not for an asterisk in a history text. This wistfulness for the past has led to a certain distortion of history which in turn has led to much of the revivalism going on these days, particularly Creedence Clearwater Revival and The Doors. It has in fact altered the substance of the music itself. The punks, while flamboyantly rejecting the soft-focus fantasies of rock from the '60s and '70s, chose for themselves yet another fantasy image, this one

Denver, Colo.

from the '50s. Suddenly, everyone in every band was wearing leather like Brando in "The Wild Ones."

The first generation grew up understanding something of rock's roots in both black and white folk musics; in blues and rhythm'n'blues, in country and rockabilly. The great blues revival in the early and mid-'60s was as much a product of this sensibility as it was due to the works of the civil rights movement.

The second generation grew up taking for granted the technology rockers in the '60s had developed. Cut off from the music's roots, this second generation nevertheless instinctively understands its inner workings. The change came when rockers started "playing" the studio, the way they once played instruments. Quickly enough, technology became rock's base. That the generation of the '70s extended its taste for technology into computers and electronic arcade games was inevitable: Pac-Man, the electronic arcade game, was rock's true evolution just as David Bowie emerged from London of the '60s.

This, of course, has led to differing expectations. For all of the banks and banks of giant amps Cream used, they were, fundamentally, a white blues band. To rock's first generation, the music was still a folk music and what it said and its texture meant had social reverberations. And this importance was overblown when the Beatles were compared to Schubert, and Mick Jagger, John Lennon, Bob Dylan or whoever was dubbed

Philadelphia, Pa.

← Rockford, Ill. →

Philadelphia, Pa.

spokesman of his generation. Still, the sense that the music *meant* something in a cultural sense, however ill-defined this meaning may have been, was still there. The Stones will

Rockford, Ill.

New York, N.Y.

never escape this particular expectation from their fans. They'll always cause waves.

The second generation doesn't look for any such meaning and, in some instances, has almost come to ridicule it. The movie version of "Sgt. Pepper" produced in the '70s treated the original music like a soundtrack for a pop-world Disneyland. Fun, pure fun. No one worried whether *Lucy In The Sky With Diamonds* actually was a secret LSD song.

Indeed, the major antagonism between the two generations has come over the question of the music's meaning. The first has tried to impose on the second not just special ideas of what rock is about but, more significantly, the sense that the music must have meaning. And in rejecting all of the first notions, the second generation has also rejected the second. It has trumpeted pop's meaninglessness and come to champion music defined by its form, not its content: disco, rockabilly, do-wha girl groups or Top 40 pop.

Simultaneous with this has been the older generation's need to review the music and the myths it grew older with, as if they were umbilically attached. Significantly enough though, this struggle between the generations has taken place within the sphere of rock. The second generation's rejection of the first took on an outlandishly, typically rock means—through the comic-book nihilism of the punks. The first generation's demythification is part of on-going rock myth as a debunking agent.

These struggles have confounded rock radio stations who are trying to program for both generations. The baby-boom generation is larger, they know, and it has far more economic clout. But the second represents the future. The same consideration confronts rock critics, those grizzled and those not.

The Stones' last tour hasn't really answered those questions as much as it's delayed any final answers. Young and old rocker showed up for it, those who only could think of the band as something particularly British and angry and challenging, and those who'd had Mick's posters on their walls since they were eight years old and who could only know that this wonderfully loud rock band called the Rolling Stones had always been there.

New York, N.Y. →

The tour's astonishing success confirmed that, for the time it lasted, a consensus between generations was reached. When the Stones played to millions, rock again became truly a public concern.

Whatever it is the Stones are all about, no one can ever replace them. They are, after all, *the* Rolling Stones.